T0007330

"I woke up the other morning and started to read this marvelous book. I stayed in bed until I had read the last page. I could not for the life of me think of anything in the world I wanted to do but read this book. I am tempted to stay in bed until Grégoire Bouillier writes another one."

—Daniel Handler

"The year's most charming oddity . . . Frank and wry, mad and graceful, Bouillier riffs on his convictions, delusions, and stray theories in [this] French pastry, performing a kind of slapstick philosophy that sheds some light on his soul."

—Troy Patterson, *Slate*, Best Books of 2006

"Darkly hilarious . . . an odyssey [that] wends its loopy way toward yes."

—*O, the Oprah Magazine*

"A mesmerizing, lyrical memoir of loves lost and unexpectedly found . . . Existential angst has rarely been as humorous or as heartbreaking."

—Jake Lamar, *People*

"[A] slim and lyrical memoir . . . What Bouillier makes of this simple setup is pure Gallic magic—a mix of hapless obsession, sophisticated abstraction, unearned righteousness and hyperarticulate self-doubt—as he tries to guess the woman's motivations and get a hold of his own feelings. The book's four short parts—phone call, preparation, party and aftermath—are small miracles of Montaigne-like self-exploration. Reading as Bouillier moves through the light and dark of love, through its forms of 'maniacal sublimation' and through its mystery, is arresting."

—*Publishers Weekly*, Starred Review

"A refreshingly odd voice . . . With its restless intelligence, *The Mystery Guest* manages to encompass all the thematic preoccupations of its touchstone, *Mrs. Dalloway*: time, fate, and the meaning of life. And unlike Ms. Woolf, Bouillier keeps us laughing . . . Bouillier's prose . . . turns every interaction between the narrator and his fellow guests into a comic meditation on the impossibility of communication . . . And then suddenly, in a stunning reversal, Bouillier sets off the depth charges he's quietly been planting throughout the book. In the end, we discover that *The Mystery Guest* isn't a symphony of missed connections after all, but a kind of hymn to possibility . . . It leaves us moved, even as we shake our heads in disbelief . . . *The Mystery Guest* [leaves] the reader in a state of grateful intoxication."

—Garth Risk Hallberg, *The Millions*

"Proust in a bottle . . . Read it, then set it on your desk. Pick it up again. Be startled. By your own scaled-down reflection most of all."

—Walter Kirn, *GQ*

"[A] perversely satisfying memoir . . . Anyone whose anxieties tend to buzz in the ear, creating a din that makes it impossible to act unself-consciously, will enjoy this slim volume. Mr. Bouillier is looking back and poking fun at himself, but the events are captured with a raw immediacy, making his parade of humiliations feel fresh and profound."

—Emily Bobrow, *New York Observer*

"A skillful blurring of art and reality is achieved in French author Bouillier's beguilingly spare 'account' of recovery from a romantic heartbreak . . . [Full of] self-aggrandizing, hilarious reflections on matters such as the ridiculous turtlenecks he has taken to wearing as a kind of Band-Aid . . . A treasure at once absurd and heartbreaking."

—*Kirkus*, Starred Review

"Pitch-perfect . . . one of the most detailed social train wrecks in contemporary letters."

—*Time Out NY*

"At once delightful and important to read."

—Susan Salter Reynolds, *Los Angeles Times*

"Somewhere out in the woeful constellation of literary comparison, a lonely satellite drifts between remote stars— *Ulysses* and *Mrs. Dalloway*, *The Stranger* and *When Harry Met Sally*—beguilingly reflecting the distant light of each. Taped to the bottom of that satellite is this perfect little book, a message to extraterrestrial intelligence that says: We are human, heartbroken, grim, and funny in our despair, yet hopeful and miracle-prone, and some of us are French."

—John Hodgman

"[A] sad, funny and vivid new memoir . . . He is an artist of the memoir form . . . Its talky, run-on, breathless tone [is] confiding and endearing . . . As *The Mystery Guest* beautifully shows—the power [of] revelation lies entirely within ourselves . . . This memoir—which is shot through with references to the literature that Bouillier loves, to Ulysses and to *Ulysses* and to Virginia Woolf—gives shape to the question of 'meaning,' whether it's illusory, whether that matters at all . . . It also gives shape to the painful yet somehow hilarious disjunction that is the residue of a shattered love affair . . . You never know, as they say, what's waiting out there for you; but if you're lucky, you might discover, at least, *The Mystery Guest*."

—Erica Wagner, *New York Times Book Review*

"Bouillier obsesses on a literary level, with eloquence, insight, Proustian perception and allusions to great works of literature (most significantly *Mrs. Dalloway*) . . . Brilliantly entertaining and at times hilarious. His biting observations have the ring of truth . . . He's not just one miserable sap trying to get over a brutal breakup. He's a self-deprecating everyman who speaks for all of us in our darkest moments of obsession and despair, clinging to any life raft—a book, a memory, a new love—to survive."

—Regan McMahon, *San Francisco Chronicle*

"A great big little book that distills the essential."

—Nelly Kaprièlian, *Les Inrockuptibles*

THE MYSTERY GUEST

THE MYSTERY GUEST

GRÉGOIRE BOUILLIER

TRANSLATED FROM THE FRENCH BY BEN TRUMAN

McNally Editions

New York

McNally Editions
134 Prince St.
New York, NY 10012

Copyright © 2004 by Éditions Allia, Paris
Translation copyright © 2024 by Ben Truman
All rights reserved
Printed in the United States of America
Originally published in 2004 by Éditions Allia,
Paris, as *L'Invité mystèr*
First McNally Editions Paperback, 2024

"De la Littérature considérée comme une tauromachie," from
Manhood by Michel Leiris, is quoted in Richard Howard's translation.

ISBN: 978-1-961341-0-50
E-book: 978-1-961341-0-67

Design by Jonathan Lippincott

1   3   5   7   9   10   8   6   4   2

To Sophie Calle

THE MYSTERY GUEST

I

It was the day Michel Leiris died. This would have been late September 1990, or else very early October; the date escapes me but never mind, I can always look it up later on. In any case it was a Sunday, because I was at home in the middle of the afternoon, and it was unseasonably cold out, and I'd gone to sleep in my clothes, wrapped up in a blanket, the way I often did when I found myself alone. In those days cold and oblivion were all I wanted. This was fine with me: one day, I knew, it would be time to rejoin the living, and that day could wait. I'd seen enough. Beings, things, landscapes . . . I had enough to ruminate on for the next century or two, that was plenty. I didn't want any more trouble.

The phone woke me up. I looked around the room; it was almost nighttime. I picked up. And right away I knew it was her. Even before I knew, I knew. It was her voice, her breath, practically her face, and with her face came a thousand happy moments: moments gilded in the sunbeams of the past, moments that had caressed my face and licked my hand, and that now hung, dead and dangling, at the end of a rope.

I sat up in my bed and in my chest my heart began pounding. I could hear it clearly, jumping up and down as if electrified, bouncing off every corner of the room, and it couldn't be an illusion, I wasn't dreaming, it was her all right, our senses don't literally lie, even though I couldn't believe my ears that it was actually her calling after all these years when she hadn't once been in touch, not once, or even sent me so much as a note. Sooner or later everything comes to pass, I thought for half a second, and on the very day that Michel Leiris should die, I thought right afterward, and the coincidence struck me as so outlandish that I almost laughed out loud, as if I'd been granted access to the inner hilarity of things, or had touched a truth so overwhelming that hysterical laughter was my only possible protection; but then again, maybe it wasn't a coincidence, and it crossed my mind that she might never have called if Michel Leiris *hadn't* died, yes, she must have heard the news, and his death must somehow have made her come back into my life. One thing might well have played obscurely into the other, or in any case I sensed a connection, and we are told that the true significance of a dream lies not in the central action but in the details, and for a long time I was convinced that the same was true in real life, or anyway, in what we call real life.

But this was no time for a philosophical debate, plus I wasn't about to start making any speeches since I could tell my voice was soft and muzzy, and instinctively I wanted to conceal the fact that her call had woken me up, and for the moment nothing else mattered, to the point that I'd have preferred sounding distant on my end, and cold and detached. Why did she have to call, not just on the day Michel Leiris died, but while I was asleep, while I was at my most defenseless and least capable of answering her call, or even of appreciating it for the miracle it was? But in the real world nothing ever occurs in an ideal form, and no doubt this is a lucky thing for humanity in general, and yet just then I'd have done anything to keep her from finding out that I'd been asleep in the middle of the afternoon—that was out of the question. It seemed like a failing on my part, it seemed churlish, somehow, given the singularity of the event, or else she might have suspected, I don't know what she might have suspected, but nothing I wanted her to know, and, *no*, my life hadn't turned into one long hibernation, and it wasn't as if I spent all my time pining away in bed all by myself ever since she'd left; quite the opposite: my life was one party after another and I was in top form, and every moment of the day was a tiptoe through the tulips, whatever she may have thought to the contrary.

The strangest thing was that I didn't remember, not even for a second, that I'd sworn never to speak to her again, or that she'd left me years before without a word, without the slightest explanation, without even a goodbye, the way people get rid of their dogs when they go on vacation, as I put it to myself at the time, and even tie the dog to a tree for good measure. I'd gone around and around my tree in both directions, climbed up into it, and spent a long time, spent millions of hours, spent whole years waiting in the void and cursing her name in the darkness, yes, cursing her, because her disappearance had taught me that I was a less exemplary person than I'd thought; but now the whole thing might as well have never happened and all that mattered was the fact of her calling, that and my certainty that this was a piece of luck and had to be seized.

I had wanted this moment so badly that I knew how it would unfold—yes, I knew what she was going to say because I'd recited the whole thing in my head. I could already see myself gently explaining that the past was the past, that the statute of limitations had elapsed, that it didn't matter anymore that she'd left me, or even *how* she'd left me. Honestly, all that was ancient history. I'd come to understand the origins of my own unhappiness, and that had nothing to do with her, and I no longer held her responsible. In this world we do the best we can, and in the end what's cruel is life itself and we're all just innocent bystanders, and don't much more horrendous things happen every day? Just this morning Michel Leiris died, and yesterday the last of the Mohawk warriors had laid down their arms, and tomorrow would bring the outbreak of some war and/or scandal that would soon be replaced in its turn, and in our case the world had turned the page must faster than I had, and it didn't exactly speak well of me that I'd taken so many years to get over her leaving; and besides, every night if you turn on the TV you can watch love conquer all in the space of an hour and a half.

Between eight forty-five and ten thirty, give or take, justice gets rendered and freedom reestablished in the hearts of men, and a name and a face are restored to humanity, and one time I even saw the entire planet Earth saved from a giant meteor in under two hours, and it's not as if I mixed up reality with fiction, no more than anybody else does, anyway, but I had gradually come to believe that I too would learn to smile again, all right maybe not in ninety minutes, but close enough. Yes, I would certainly learn to smile again in a comparable length of time; it had been nothing, and the really crazy thing was how long it took me to assimilate the fact of her leaving, and now I considered it a blessing, how callous she'd been. At least it showed a certain panache, and not every love story leaves a scar to prove that it existed, and I'd come to see it her way, yes, the truth was she'd only been trying to save herself; things had become so unbearable between us, she was acting on the survival instinct. And she was sorry, she said she was sorry and she quietly asked me to forgive her and I wanted to cry, tears actually welled up in my eyes, when she wondered aloud, yet again, how she could have left me the way she did, from one day to the next, after the four years we'd spent living together, after all we'd been through, all we'd shared; but she'd had no choice and she was in so much pain back then, and she'd been so young and she felt so guilty, without knowing why; she went around feeling guilty all the time, and I'd never know just how guilty she felt, and maybe it was society's fault, or her family's, or maybe the blame lay somewhere else entirely, she didn't know, but in the end she just took the first opportunity that came along: she went off with the first guy who'd have her, and he was nice to her, and he loved her, and she loved him too, despite his age and the fact that he was short, and now they had a little girl, and she was relieved that I was taking it so well. I'd laugh, she said, but she had been convinced that I had turned into a bum and when she was on the bus she'd look out the window at the public benches expecting to see me; she was so sure things had gone badly for me, and it scared her, and for years she'd been afraid of bumping into me, and I couldn't imagine how long it had taken her just to work up the nerve to call, and it hadn't been easy tracking me down either, and in the end she said again how sorry she was and she hoped I could forgive her. I had to understand, it was important to her, and I did understand, I understood everything, and I forgave her because in my dreams I was a forgiving person; I was magnanimous, and, besides, what else could I say or do?

This time, though, it was her voice; I wasn't dealing with some chimera that I'd invented to fill the void; I wasn't salving my wounds, as they say. This time I was going to hear her version, and she was actually going to apologize and acknowledge what had taken place, and pass a gentle hand over my eyes, so that I could look upon other sights, proceed to the next world, and love again with no regrets, yes, she owed me an explanation, or at any rate she owed me *something*; something that would seal the tomb, R.I.P., and we'd speak of it no more, and all would be redeemed, and the weeds and nettles would be mowed down within me. Why else would she have called? I wanted to know the truth and the meaning of what had happened and to be made light again, and I was prepared.

But she hadn't called to talk about the past; she didn't mention the past, much less clear things up the way I'd hoped, and my heart, which had leapt at the prospect and danced with joy, so that I'd felt it floating high above me, came plummeting back into the shadows and burrowed down in shame when I realized that she was calling to invite me to a party, and that this was the only reason she'd called, to invite me to a party, and must we really go through life pinching ourselves at every new calamity? It was going to be a big party, she added, and she was counting on me, it was important, she'd consider it a favor, and she gave a little laugh on her end of the line while silently I confirmed that the only reason she had called after all these years was to invite me to a party, as if it were nothing and time had laid waste to everything, as if Michel Leiris were still among us.

I closed my eyes, I listened. This was a birthday celebration for her husband's best friend, that is, the best friend of the man who'd become her husband and the father of her daughter, yes, every year Sophie, that was the friend's name; she was a "contemporary artist"—she said this in quotes—maybe I'd heard of her, yes exactly, Sophie Calle, the one who followed people around in the street, anyway, every year this friend had a birthday party and invited as many people as she was years old plus a "mystery guest" who stood for the year she was about to live, and this year Sophie had charged *her* with supplying the anonymous stranger and she couldn't say no, and so she'd thought of me, and she laughed again, and that's why she called.

On my end I remained impassive. I was an iron bar. Clearly I was the only person she could find who would go along with this masquerade of hers, and since nobody had heard of me I must have seemed the perfect candidate for the job, and it occurred to me that this mission must have held some strange appeal for her if she was ready to sweep aside all the obvious objections raised by our shared history and pick up the phone for the sole purpose of inviting me to a party, unless she were acting out of pure disinterestedness, or was this the only pretext she could find for seeing me again—wait, did she want to see me again? Anything was possible. But why should she need a pretext? All she had to do was call and say "Could we get together" or "I'd like to get together" or better yet "Would you like to get together?" and then her tone would have acknowledged what had existed between us and what a thousand years could never efface, and I'd have come running, my heart would have come running. But to invite me to a party? How dare she? It was out of the question, and I'd been humiliated enough, and yet in a voice that was practically chipper, even so, I heard myself accept her invitation. Yes, I'd be her "mystery guest," consider it done, I'd be there, never fear, even as I gnashed my teeth with every fiber of my being. She sounded oddly relieved, and no sooner had I spoken than once again her voice took on the sweetness of forget-me-nots, and I jotted down the time and address of the party; then, without my knowing exactly how it happened, she'd already hung up, not that we had anything left to say that could have been said on the phone.

My hand was shaking as I hung up, and the room was silent, and the air was livid, and the telephone sat there smirking on the bed, and in my rage I lobbed it across the room, but it didn't even break, and for whole seconds I sat there listening to the dial tone in the dark, and that was even worse; so I got up to put the phone back where it belonged and hang it up, then I didn't know what to do, so I walked from one end of the apartment to the other, and that didn't take long, and this was the limit, this was the bouquet, yes, all I could think to say was "*C'est le bouquet*. This latest, this really is the bouquet," and for a good hour I paced the apartment repeating those words out loud as if they were the sum total of my vocabulary, and, at the same time, I felt a sort of exaltation tingling in my veins, and I was jubilant despite myself because the meeting she'd owed me all these years was finally coming to pass, and for that I didn't mind making a fool of myself at some fashionable party, I'd have put up with much worse if that's what it took to see her again, so she'd finally give me an explanation and cut the leash that bound me to her disappearance and put an end, once and for all, to this strangulation, and I wanted answers. The rest of my life depended on this party, that much I knew, and that night I dreamed of a horse trampling a tailcoat in the dust.

II

The next day and the days that followed were unspeakable. Her call had plunged me into the sort of hellish turpitude I thought I had put behind me, and which all of a sudden I hadn't, and I found myself returning to the dark thoughts that I thought I had banished, and once again I was prey to the same old grinning demons, as if all my efforts to break free and get on with my life had been in vain, as if everything was always in vain, and I felt like tearing the skin off my face. And yet for ages I'd considered ours a "closed case," as they say, and when I went to get bread at the bakery, my thoughts didn't automatically turn to her, and there were plenty of other signs that I was over her, as they say, that I'd turned a corner, as they say, and even resurfaced, the way people always manage to do, more or less, albeit at the cost of some irreversible modification of their being or some disastrous transformation of the self, a visible change in the lips or shoulders or hair or, more unmistakably, in the depths of their eyes, in their walk or the way they laugh or talk or hold themselves, and all you have to do is look around to see for yourself.

Sometimes, though, the change is in how they dress: in my case, since I'd always detested turtleneck undershirts and loathed the men who wore them, considering these the most detestable men on the planet and the phoniest kind of dandy with, as they say, the cheesiest kind of collar, for this very reason, I started wearing turtleneck undershirts after she left me and never, so to speak, dropped the habit, which somehow must have made me feel as though no one would ever drop *me*, but, in any case, they had erupted into my life without my noticing, and then it was too late; those fateful turtleneck undershirts had gotten hold of, had flung themselves onto, my existence, and I no longer knew the feeling of the wind on the back of my neck, so inextricable from the feeling of freedom itself; but who cared if that was the price I had to pay, I told myself, who cared, who doesn't go around in some kind of straitjacket or other? In the end, we all spend our lives falling away from ourselves and disappearing behind our self-denials. Who was I to complain? Others had it worse, I consoled myself, and all around me I observed people wrapped up in bandages much gaudier than my own, yes, I wasn't such a basket case, I told myself, finally I'd found a viable way of moving through the world and concealing my condition, and once again I could fake it around other people the way they faked it around me, and this was actually going amazingly well; I was sailing through life with impunity and felt altogether relaxed, and I'd even met somebody new.

Yes, despite my turtleneck undershirts a woman had taken an interest in me, of late, and to my shock my turtleneck undershirts didn't put her off, although most women feel an instinctive, to my mind completely legitimate, revulsion for men who wear turtleneck undershirts—unless for some reason they find them attractive, but I gave those women a wide berth then and still do, and in any case she wasn't one of those; she just didn't seem to notice my sartorial neurosis, for which I was extremely grateful, though at the same time I found it exasperating, even horrific, the fact that my turtleneck undershirts never disgusted her, not even a little bit, not for so much as an hour, when disgust would have made me feel less alone and would have lightened my burden, and the certainty that she loved me *in a state of full disclosure* would have enhanced the value of her affections then and there. But no, she didn't seem aware of any deeper meanings hidden in my wearing of turtleneck undershirts, and so I remained at her side, misunderstood and furious and conflicted, and deep down, in the most odious and unfair way, I blamed her for putting up with my turtleneck undershirts when it was exactly her indifference to them that had first endeared her to me. Everything about us is so twisted; isn't every stroke of luck actually a trap?

It's the worst thing that could happen to me, I told her. The worst because I'm never free and because I seem to be what I'm not and never was and would never have *become* except by force of circumstance, as they say, and while I was saying all this, she fell into a habit she had of stroking her right cheek, as if she were trying to wipe away a trace of I don't know what: some irritant that wouldn't go away, a slap that she couldn't forget no matter how much she rubbed, a slap that had left her seeming hesitant and tongue-tied; but when I pointed out that she hadn't always rubbed at her face that way, she laughed and shrugged and claimed that I was making a mountain out of a molehill, as they say, and she insisted that this cheek-rubbing of hers was no more than a harmless tic, although she couldn't stop doing it, and I didn't press the point because I didn't want to spoil the night or poison the mood and, in any case, none of this would have happened if years before that other person hadn't left me from one day to the next without a word, without the slightest explanation, etc., and all things considered I preferred to sleep in the afternoon when I was alone, and that's when she'd called and asked me to come to a "big party," and on walls all over the city big posters were announcing the opening of *Die Hard*, and I was in despair.

At the same time the headlines in the newsstands were all full of German reunification, and *Best* featured "The Cure: Reintegration" on its cover while *Guitare et Claviers* featured "Rita Mitsouko Remixed," and the whole world seemed in a frenzy to recycle the past, as if to stride that much more blithely into the third millennium, and to settle old accounts before opening any new ones, and so I told myself that there was nothing random about her call, that it was part of the march of history, yes, somehow it had more to do with history than I realized, and we are all products of our environment. That might explain it. Because amid the chaos of all my emotions and sensations, I was still trying to solve what I took to be the mystery of her call, yes, I considered it a riddle, an offense to reason, and I just didn't get it. What could have possessed her? The mind boggled.

Was she bent on my complete and utter destruction? Was this some sort of *plot*? But too much water had passed under the bridge, as they say, for her to be seeking revenge after all these years, and besides, as far as I could tell, she had nothing *to* avenge, and so that didn't make any sense; there had to be some other explanation. Presumably she had access to the same basic human emotions as anybody else, and I no longer knew what to think. My head was one big wound, and I twisted it around in my turtleneck undershirt trying to see what exactly I was missing, because there had to be a meaning in there somewhere, or else the jig, as they say, was up and civilization was just another lie, a lie it wasn't even worth pretending to believe in anymore in the so-called civilized countries of the world, and late one afternoon I stepped to the very edge of the curb as the traffic came barreling down the boulevard.

But having survived her disappearance, I would not let it be said that her reappearance had done me in. I refused to give up; absurdly, instinctively, I wanted to understand, and this desire—to understand—was what I clung to, and this alone kept me going and kept me human. Then suddenly it struck me that she'd called late on a Sunday afternoon and that it was also a Sunday when she left me, also in the middle of the afternoon, and this couldn't be a coincidence. That much I knew, it wasn't a coincidence. How could it be a coincidence? Something else had to be going on. It was too perfect. I couldn't get past it. Yes, that was the thing, that was the truth; it couldn't have been more obvious: by calling me on that day of the week, at that time of day, she had contrived to pick up the thread of our relationship exactly where it had been severed, and she was telling me that all the intervening years since she'd left me had lasted no more than a handful of seconds, and this changed everything. Suddenly time was no longer an issue, and there had been nothing final about her disappearance either, and so our love had never ceased to exist and was immortal and all the rest was straw in the wind, and this stuff about the party was a pretext, or even a lure, because if all she'd wanted was to invite me to a party, she could have called on a Monday morning or a Friday evening or on a Thursday at noon, but she'd certainly never have called late in the afternoon on a Sunday, and miracles do occur between people who've been in love. Secretly I rejoiced; I was all atremble, and her call, which had seemed to me the last word in brutality, now made sense, the clearest and most overwhelming kind of sense. Reality always gives us some loophole by which to save us from itself.

For once, no one could say I was overthinking. Appearances don't lie, I told myself, they mean what they mean and you don't need to look behind them or anywhere else but *at* them, and I was exultant, and the reasons for her call seemed clearer and clearer and more and more magnificent, and really they had nothing to do with her. Because it wasn't as if she had *planned* to call me late on a Sunday afternoon and send me a coded message, no one would be so devious, and devious to what end? I asked myself, no,

one had to posit some other force—I didn't know what
to call it—that could find no other way to express itself,
no other way to signal me, and which, with a will of its
own, had induced her to pick up the phone and enter my
number at this one moment, of all the possible moments,
a moment whose meaning I alone could understand, yes, I
was convinced and it had to be the case that, for a reason as
yet unknown but that might have had something to do with
the death of Michel Leiris, this force had unleashed something deep inside her, and she'd seized on the job of finding
a "mystery guest" in order to put out her hand and wave a
handkerchief like a prisoner in her tower, with absolute trust
that, in spite of everything, I would perceive the call within
the call. How else could you explain her total silence over
all these years, that is, without imagining some counterspell
that finally broke the curse? Why else, when she called, did
she make no reference to the past, the way anybody would
do under the circumstances, since it would be the most
natural thing *to* do, and this made it clear that she wasn't in
a normal frame of mind and was acting in the grip of some
larger force and was its plaything. A psychoanalyst would
surely have spoken of the unconscious, but I told myself that
this force was nothing more or less than our love, which
beyond our personalities and everything that separated us
and got in our way, had never ceased to exist and even had a
life of its own, and that surpassed us, and in any case, from
the very beginning, what bound us together had never been
merely terrestrial in nature. I thought of how certain comets
return cyclically to Earth after having ventured to the ends
of the universe, and I was utterly convinced that our love

was returning, in just the same way, to orbit our two lives after having spent all these years flung into a distant and frozen past; no doubt the comet would pass closest to us at the time of this party, which was scheduled to take place Saturday, October 13, 1990, and the perfection of all these multiples of three now struck me as propitious, albeit fairly random in comparison to the rest, and I'm not making any of this up; my imagination is better than that.

Any lingering doubts had melted away: I was going to the party. How could I not? Such a confluence would take decades to come again, if it ever did. How could I pass up the chance to receive her secret message? I wanted to hold this love of ours in my arms one last time and feel the vertigo of it, which was more than just her or me. At the same time, I was berating myself for being an idiot, for being crazy—no, for being an idiot—and I was consumed with self-mockery; I was just a dime-store Don Quixote looking for trouble, and trouble was what I'd find. What was the matter with me? Despair had an energy of its own, and so I'd created this world all of my own where I got to be the star, and now I was going to see things for what they were; this party would be the death of all my illusions, it would tear me to shreds, and I'd never get over it, and couldn't I see the trap I was falling into? Couldn't I see she was making a fool of me? Yes, the whole world was going to burst out laughing, and I was a nothing and didn't matter to anyone and had nothing to look forward to but more disaster and humiliation and bitterness, just like that general Aoun, besieged in Beirut, running out of time and shouting his defiance from what was clearly a pile of ruins; but I stopped up my ears and refused to hear my own protestations, in which I recognized the anguished voices of my mother and father and my grandparents and great-grandparents and all my forbears, and everyone else who had ever been born and lived since Biblical times, all of them repeating uselessly that they'd told me so, that I shouldn't come complaining to them when I was reduced to a wandering shade, and I ignored them; I had a rendez-vous—I might not know with what, exactly, but a ren-dezvous all the same, and that was what mattered, and nothing could change my mind or weaken my resolve, for the moment was approaching when her disappearance, which remained a great mystery to me, would once and for all be elucidated. I'd always known I must somehow be overlooking the real reason she left, since nobody leaves a person from one day to the next without a highly specific and in the end very particular reason, and even the most miserable wife at least says goodbye when she leaves, and there had to be more going on here, and I had to know what it was, and then I myself would be elucidated, and the doom of the turtleneck undershirts would be at an end.

For all my certainty, I felt feverish and uneasy and was in a state of absolute disgust and impotent rage whenever I thought about showing up at this party to play the part of a sentimental curiosity and a stuffed monkey and a dwarf to be tossed as far as possible to beat some record the exact nature of which eluded me. In Flint, Michigan, hadn't the regional managers of General Motors thrown a big party to console everyone who had been laid off after the "outsourcing" of one of their plants, and on the grounds of an immense estate overlooking the town weren't the unemployed paid to act the part of living statues, to hold a pose while cigar-smoking men in tuxedos and women in evening gowns milled around sipping California champagne? I thought of Baudelaire demolishing the Belgians, and of Rimbaud insulting the scribblers of his day, and of Thomas Bernhard and Artaud and Alfieri, and of Paul sending off his epistles, and I took joy in their existence; they made me feel less alone, and I swelled up with their examples as if somehow I shared in their refusals to be demeaned and unmanned and denatured, as if now it were my turn to unmask an era and its most prominent personalities, yes, I too wanted to leap out from the ranks of these assassins and their cronies. Was I not after all the "mystery guest"? They had no idea just what a mystery guest I was going to be, because I was thirty years old, and the time had come to proclaim my existence on Earth and, no, it was neither empty nor pointless, and the bleakest moment was exactly when the tide would turn, I told myself, when no one was expecting it, and like a jack-in-the-box I'd grab at the chance they offered me and defeat them so completely they'd have to start walking around on their hands.*

·

---

* An untranslatable pun: *montrer qu'ils avaient tellement baissé les bras qu'ils marchaient desormais sur les mains.* (All footnotes are the translator's.)

To say I was afraid would be an understatement. The closer I came to the day and the hour of my rendezvous, or, as I grimly called it, my surrender,* the more I felt that I was hurtling toward my own destruction for no reason and the more I felt my strength failing and my determination wavering and the certainty that I would lay bare "the figure in the carpet" melting away into doubt, so great was the task before me, a task that I would have to perform all by myself. Ulysses at least had his son with him and the swineherd Eumaeus and that other one, the cowherd, and an old serving woman, and most of all Athena, to help him take on the suitors and win Penelope back; I would have no companions or allies, and the opposite of courage isn't cowardice but discouragement, at least in French. Such thoughts preyed on my nerves night and day, and on whatever my nerves were connected to, and I kept vacillating, trying on every heroic guise I could think of before gloomily donning that of the mystery guest, tricking myself out in it as if in some grotesque suit of armor, and tarring myself with that title. As I waited for reality to render its verdict, I thought, in moments of nervous calm and renewed tenderness, of Alceste giving his hand to Célimène when she finds herself humiliated at the end of Act V; but then I'd think of Humbert Humbert giving money to his beloved Lolita, now reduced to a wretched double of her own mother, and how in the end, the Consul dies a pitiful death at the foot of his volcano after he's been reunited with his beloved Yvonne. What sort of as-yet-unwritten

---

* Another pun: *le jour et l'heure de me rendre à cette soirée et de me rendre tout court.*

reunion awaited me? What revelations and cruelties and humiliations would be mine?

Then my euphoria faded, and I began to lash myself again and shout that I refused to play such a part, no, never, who did they think they were, and who did they think I was? I had a name and they couldn't take *that* away from me along with everything else, and, yes, I needed to protect myself once in a while; even self-laceration has its limits, and I couldn't always be prey to other people and their desires and their obscure machinations. I was going to show them who I was, they'd see, the world would see, the entire world, and in the first place, I wasn't going to show up empty-handed. This was a birthday, after all, and I hadn't forgotten; I spent hours racking my brain to figure out what a "mystery guest" ought to give someone he's never met who is, moreover, a "contemporary artist," and supposedly a "well-known contemporary artist," and this added to my exasperation and resentment and made me raise the bar even higher, as they say. But I couldn't come up with any idea for a gift, and I was tearing my hair out, pacing the length of my bedroom for the thousandth time, and I didn't have any money, but I mean I *really* didn't have any money, to the point that I was wearing shoes I'd bought secondhand at the flea market in Clignancourt. But what did money and shoes have to do with it when the whole situation vitiated the very idea of the gift, and of the connection the gift creates between two individuals beyond the object being given? I muttered to myself—unless the thing to do was to find the most transcendent present of them all, I said to myself, the one present that could symbolize The Gift as such, independent of whoever happened to receive it or be its bearer, yes, maybe this woman Sophie meant for the "mystery guest" to arrive at the highest possible conception of present-hood. Was that what she had in mind? I wandered the streets and walked up and down the avenues with my nose glued to the windows, as they say; but wherever I looked, all I saw was merchandise and more merchandise and nothing with any value except the value assigned to each thing in its turn by society, and nowhere I looked did any object give me the feeling that it embodied anything but profit and gain, and in all directions lay products that expressed nothing but an idea that was degraded and even contrary, not to say hostile, to that of the gift, and I didn't want to show up to that party holding a present whose magic would last no longer than it took to remove the shiny paper and the bow. All of a sudden I understood why, in our societies, presents always come wrapped: not to create an effect of surprise, but to conceal our knowledge that the surprise is a lie, and this knowledge comes back to us, inevitably, every time we get a present, yes, we open it, and in that split second we know we're about to be swindled, feel a tingle of disgust and sadness, and hurry to smile and say thank you so as to suppress, in the deepest part of our being, the annoyance of never once in our lives being given something truly unexpected, and this joy, forever disappointed, remains inscrutable to us.

For a second I thought I might give her a book by Michel Leiris. At least it would beat flowers or candy, I told myself, yes, however disappointing and unprepossessing a solution it might be, it also struck me as the least bad option, and for a long time now haven't all of our choices been made "by default" or "faute de mieux" and according to the logic of the lesser evil, as if nothing now was able to win our full and total and enthusiastic support. How long must we go on economizing in the expression of our desires? Then it hit me: wine! Of course, why hadn't I thought of it sooner? Nothing could be more perfect, I'd found the answer, no need to look further, I'd give her wine, a very great bottle of wine, the oldest and most expensive wine I could get, and this idea felt prodigious, as if coming from something deep within me, deep and ancient; it brought together all my strengths and my desires until it became immense and glorious, and it was a feeling too big to hold inside, and I started laughing there in the street, yes, if they wanted my blood, I thundered silently, at least it would be vintage, and of an excellent year, and they could drink it in remembrance of me, and wasn't Christ himself a model "mystery guest"? The more time I spent with this idea, the more carried away and intoxicated I became, and the more it seemed to sum up, in itself, every truly positive choice that I could imagine, and in a wine shop in Saint-Lazare I found a 1964 Margaux, I remember very clearly, it was the nicest bottle they had, and it was way over my budget, and I exulted and pranced around in front of the sales clerk, who looked at me with suspicion, and even a degree of concern, yes, I wanted to sacrifice everything I had, and to shame them by throwing myself on their pyre, and we'd see what they were made of and whether they had brought presents that were over their budgets; we'd have a potlatch, and for once put all social chicanery aside, and we'd find out who was ready to sacrifice the most for his desire. The bottle cost much more than my rent and that didn't matter, on the contrary, the barrel was tapped, as they say, the die was cast, and the rent could wait, and in fact it did. When I left the shop I carried my bottle in its tissue paper as if it were a talisman, and the city seemed to have changed its aspect and transformed into a cheerful farce, and I felt big enough to cross outside the crosswalk and stop the cars with a glance to contend with their bumpers and their bodies of steel; no longer would the distress and indigence of the world force indigence and distress upon me; no longer would my own opulence require me to beg, I recited to myself, for in that moment I felt that I had earned the right to quote Hölderlin, a thing that doesn't happen every day.

How much had changed since her phone call! I had been rudderless and now I had a mission, and I was no longer alone, for I contained multitudes, and I was on my way, the time had come, and to hell with the expense, I told myself, calling a cab to take me to the party as if I were indulging in one last cigarette. Leaning my head against the rear door, my hands not once letting go of the '64 Margaux in my lap but brooding over it like an egg, I watched the lights and shadows go by out the

GRÉGOIRE BOUILLIER

window, and I remembered how everything started with
the death of Michel Leiris, and, since that time, I had
been apprised, as they say, that hundreds of thousands
of Germans had been reunited and sung "Ode to Joy" in
front of the Reichstag, and riots had broken out in Vaulx-
en-Velin, and in Rwanda rebels had invaded the north,
and an anthropologist had confirmed that social ties
between baboons were based on affection, and the Bayeux
Tapestry might not date from the eleventh century, since
nobody cooked with brochettes before the 1700s, and an
attack in Jerusalem's Mosque Square had left twenty dead
while, at the same time, three climbers had conquered
Mount Everest. I had taken note of all of these items in
a little notebook in order to remember them later on,
for that entire week I never lost the conviction that I
was taking part in world events and was connected in
some tiny invisible way to everything happening everywhere, and I closed my eyes in the cab and concentrated
and tried mentally to reconstruct the chain in which I
formed one link; but all I could manage was rioters roast-
ing something-or-other with brochettes in Jerusalem for
a bunch of Beethoven-singing baboons, or the equiva-
lent, yes, despite my best efforts, all the news that had
transpired, as they say, over the past week, ended up as a
string of interchangeable words, signifying nothing but
their own accumulation, and in the end reality was no
more than an absurd fiction, terrifying in its absurdity,
and wasn't this exactly the way it was presented? Then
suddenly I remembered that the space probe *Ulysses* had
taken off the day before, or two days before, for the sun,

and if I understood correctly, this was the first time that a man-made object was going to leave the plane of Earth's orbit and those of all the other planets and leave our solar system, and that wasn't nothing, and I even found myself praying that the little probe would have a smooth flight to wherever it was going, yes, here finally was an event that seemed to speak to my condition, here finally was news that gave me a sign and encouraged me instead of crushing and terrorizing me and filling me with disgust and impotence, and I suddenly felt peaceful and self-assured, as if I'd been nourished by all the efforts of the most creative brains on the planet, and in the shadows I began to smile, looking down at the Margaux, and I made sure it wasn't jiggling around too much in my lap. At this point the driver ventured that it was chilly for its being so early in October, and you just couldn't tell about the weather nowadays. I didn't feel like talking, but he did, and he was in a confiding mood, and he told me that his wife had left him two years before and that he had lost seventeen kilos, even he couldn't believe it, seventeen kilos, and he chuckled in solitary bewilderment as if he had performed some stupendous feat, and I said maybe that's how much his wife weighed to him, seventeen kilos, and he looked at me in the rearview mirror; he'd never thought about it that way or considered the possibility that love could not only *be* a weight, but could have one, too, and I revealed that, for my part, I had been wearing turtleneck undershirts, so we were even, but I could tell he found my case trivial compared to his, and he just nodded and turned up the volume on the radio just as a voice introduced the last live recording from "the immortal Barbara," and for what seemed like forever, all I could think of was how the black eagle was back and had come out of nowhere, and each of us has his own mystery guest, and the fare came to nearly one hundred francs, in the currency of the time.*

<hr />

* Bouillier is quoting "L'Aigle noir," signature hit of the singer-songwriter known as Barbara (1930–1997).

III

She wasn't the one who opened the door. She didn't appear as on the first day, sculpted in the light from the party, and we didn't stand there looking at each other in silence, too moved to speak, while our eyes drank in what they had been missing for so long and the old magic stirred again and cast its web, and a single smile passed from her lips to mine like a kiss that had never come to an end. In actuality, nobody came to the door. The place where the taxi had dropped me off was forbidding, across from a train track surmounted by giant concrete panels that were obviously supposed to muffle the noise of the trains, and the only human presence was that of the streetlights, which revealed a deserted corner and which glowed in the cold with dim, reluctant halos. I don't know how long I stood there, tapping my foot on the pavement, freezing and at a loss, in front of a small unpainted metal door that seemed to have been cut out of the much larger door of a garage or abandoned factory. There was no way to guess what was going on behind that steel or what might await me once I crossed the threshold, and I wanted to turn tail, as they say, and set out for a better, less arduous life; I had no business in this neighborhood, I told myself, none of it made any sense, and even the intercom refused to cooperate, and it took me several minutes to figure out that you had to scroll through a list of names on this greenish little screen before it displayed the name Sophie Calle. In the end, nothing was happening the way I'd imagined. Not

that I'd formed a precise idea of what awaited me when
I arrived, but at least in my mind it hadn't been so chilly
and my fingers weren't numb from clutching the bottle of
Margaux, and who cared about intercoms or streetlights?
Yes, in my mind I'd showed up at the party, and there it
all was: I was right in the thick of it, as they say, without
any big surprises or interference; but this was not the way
events were tending, not at all, and suddenly I felt very
sober, after all the ideas and fireworks and sparklers I'd had
going off in me for the past two weeks, as if the world in
all its heaviness had grabbed me by the hand, as if it were
trying to drag me back down into its slough of despond,
and no doubt at that very moment the probe *Ulysses* was
encountering some problem of its own. But it hardly made
sense to back out now, and anyway there was no more time
for either procrastination or deliberation over whether to
give up or go on. I would have my answer soon enough, I
muttered, and I screwed up my courage, as they say, and
I took a deep breath, and, with an air of ceremony that
made even me smile, I pressed the button on the intercom,
but nothing happened, no bell rang, and my act had no
echo, as if it hadn't tripped a switch and hadn't even taken
place, as if I didn't exist myself, and for a split second
everything went wavy before my eyes and started to sink.
How could that silence reign on uninterrupted when everything in me was shouting that I had just accomplished
something resounding? There had to be some mistake,
reality couldn't be so completely at odds with what I felt,
the world couldn't be so perverse as to call into question
the simple ringing of a doorbell, it couldn't be as diabolical

as that, and I pressed the button on the intercom again, in the mad hope that somewhere something was ringing and that someone would hear it, and it crossed my mind that a century earlier no one could have imagined that one day a human being would be reduced to such an outlandish hope; but once again there was nothing, everything was still, and I began to count the seconds without noticing that they were actually the beats of my racing heart, while my eyes lingered on the white paint that was peeling at the edges of the intercom, and for a brief instant, I began contemplating the shapes that were born of this degradation, recognizing the form of a woman wearing a hat, or possibly it was a face in profile, and in the end it was looking more like a clump of clouds—when suddenly the door unlocked with a flat, electric buzz, and a moment later, guided by bursts of talk that grew more distinct as I went, I crossed a small vegetable garden, which led to what seemed to be an abandoned factory converted into an artist's loft, and a bay window stretching across the entire façade revealed that the party was already in full swing, as they say, and through the glass, I recognized her silhouette in the distance, and I saw her before she saw me.

No doubt about it: it was her, and she was standing with two men and one was cackling and she was starting to smile, too, and she hid her mouth with her hand the way, it came back to me, she always used to do, and her hair was as blond as I remembered but it was shorter now, or styled differently, I couldn't tell which, and although I'd expected to feel overwhelmed, there was nothing, or, at least, nothing I could access. The earth didn't shake, and it was even disconcerting how completely familiar it was to have her standing there and, at the same time, how incongruous, and I pushed open the sliding door, taking care not to bump the Margaux. Seeing me come out of the cold a woman turned and smiled, and I smiled back without failing to notice her small breasts, and from this moment on, everything proceeded as if someone else were acting in my place, yes, I distinctly felt that when I entered this room, I was also entering the body of a character who hadn't been there a second ago and who now took up the baton and composed my features so as to protect me and defend me from the eyes of the other attendees and who would keep me from looking ridiculous and, at the same time, would prevent me from making a scene or committing the slightest indiscretion or even faux pas; yes, against my will a metamorphosis had taken place, to my advantage and disadvantage, and it was as if I had no inner life now, except in fits and starts, and there was nothing left to be done about it, and I cursed my sense of propriety and told myself I could wait, yes, let them test me and I'd explode the masquerade, nothing had been signed, as they say, and I took off my coat in the manner of someone who can walk into any room and take off his coat, and I rolled it into a ball and deposited it beside a magnificent bouquet of white and red roses that were exploding out of a vase placed right there on the floor, and this bouquet took up a really incredible amount of space, it occurred to me—maybe not as much space as *The Odyssey* took up in my life, but close—and in spite of myself I started counting the roses, as if I needed to know, right then, how many were in that vase, so at least one thing about my situation would not remain unknown to me, yes, quite often to know *something* is all it takes to feel that one *knows* something, and so to be soothed. In the end there were thirty-seven roses, and no doubt this was the number of birthday candles that would later be extinguished, and at the thought of seeing a cake brought in and people singing "Happy Birthday," I felt defeated before the fact.

No one was paying any attention to me, and everything happened exactly the way it does in real life: enigmatically, but not in any clear or intelligible way, and I lit a cigarette to occupy much more than just my hands or lungs, and I mingled in the party with an air of detachment, as they say. I was sure that everyone must already have noticed my turtleneck undershirt and I plunged straight ahead without meeting anyone's eye and made a beeline for a certain corner as if I knew exactly where I was going, as if it were the easiest thing in the world, and it wasn't a bad corner to have chosen because there, underneath a large iron staircase leading up to the second floor, I found a nook where I could observe everything without being noticed or ambushed from behind, and for the moment the hardest part seemed to be over, and only then did I dare to look up and take in my surroundings.

•

The room was immense, and in the middle there was a table so big that it seemed to be driving the walls farther and farther out of its way, and the place settings went on for kilometers, and the white tablecloth was made up of multiple dazzling sheets, like a bridal train under the harshness of the track lights overhead, and chairs and stools were drawn up all around the table, and at the foot of the staircase a stuffed cat was captured mid-pounce and would never touch down again, and behind it a pink flamingo was standing on one leg, and everything was cheerful and festive; all around me men and women were chatting and talking and milling around, and some were on their way out while others were arriving, and many wore black and were smoking, and some were sitting with their elbows on the table and picking at little plates of hors d'oeuvres and saucisson, and most held a glass of champagne. One woman was demanding that they put on some Spanish music, while a man in a white panama hat was sulking in a corner. It was a party all right; it was a party like any good party, and in one sense this was a relief, and at the same time I wanted to scream, even as I beamed a series of fake smiles into the middle distance. Then a woman slipped and nearly fell as she was carrying a large platter to the table, and a bit of slapstick ensued that drew everyone's attention, heads turned. And that's when she saw me; her gaze crossed the room and stopped where I was, and she interrupted the man who'd been laughing a minute before, she put her hand on his arm and murmured in his ear, and he looked my way as she left his side and approached me,

and the fact that the man was following her with his eyes
kept me from savoring this moment, which I'd promised
myself as recompense, yes, he was ruining everything, but
no more than everything else did in the end, and I held
perfectly still, smiling and betraying no emotion even as
I watched her come toward me. She was very beautiful;
I had forgotten just how beautiful she was, and at the
same time I didn't remember her possessing quite this
sort of beauty, or having ever worn this dress, which left
her shoulders bare and made her immediately desirable
and, so to speak, sexual, to the point that as she walked
by, neither men nor women could keep from eyeing her,
and for a split second a thousand thoughts and feelings
washed over me, all tending toward the question of
whether she had chosen this dress for my sake, to charm
me and bring me to my knees, as they say, or whether she
was trying to make me understand that now she partook
of another world and the desires of another man. Both
scenarios were possible, and possibly all she wanted was
to exercise her powers of seduction over everyone and no
one in particular, yes, I know as well as anyone else that
a woman doesn't choose her clothes at random, especially
not under circumstances like these, but whatever inten-
tions her outfit may have revealed were lost in the folds
of her dress, and I felt everything crashing together inside
me, as if only her enchantment was holding me upright,
as if there were nothing in sight to hang onto, and I felt
a trapdoor fall open under my feet when all at once she
loomed up before me and, as if it were the most natural
thing in the world, leaned in to kiss my cheek, and *this*

was the last straw. This familiarity was shocking, it was obscene, it was nonsense, as if our history could ever, even conceivably, degenerate into, what should I call it, friendliness? Camaraderie? It was unthinkable, she could save her blandishments and empty hellos for other men; otherwise love had no meaning, and our life together had never taken place, and she herself did not exist, and in that one moment I could have torn her face right off and trampled it on the floor, and how could she blame me, no, it wasn't acceptable that what had connected us, and still did connect us, in spite of everything, should molder away into petty, commonplace, reasonable feelings. What we had between us was different, and we deserved better, and what begins in beauty can only end in beauty, as they say, or otherwise how come Michel Leiris had died and what was the point of asking me to this party? Or maybe all she'd wanted was to catch my scent, surreptitiously, after all these years, and feel the touch of her skin against mine without any risk of reproach, yes, and in the end something in her manner may have left some room for hope, but in any case it was too late; I had already given her a kiss on the cheek, closing my eyes and clenching my fists and fighting the desire to seek out her lips and find and part them and feel her tongue, and drown the way I used to do, and in order to stop the charade as fast as I could, I pressed the bottle into her hands, saying "From the mystery guest," and I would not wish it on anyone ever to smile the way I smiled.

•

I have no memory of the other words we exchanged, none at all, I was too busy listening to her face, and it was all I could hear, yes, everything was inscribed in the hollows where her cheeks used to be, where they had melted away and disappeared, as if with the last faded remnants of her childhood, and left a burnt husk, that's the only word for it, and I could hardly bear to look her in the face; I felt sorry despite myself and close to tears, and it hit me how much she must have been through and put up with, and I turned my head to keep her from reading the sadness in my eyes, which was larger than us two, and it struck me that she must have noticed certain things about me as well, things she was keeping to herself, and I couldn't have been exactly a sight for sore eyes, and was every second of this party going to be an ordeal, and an affront, and a calvary of endless disillusionment? For she had taken the bottle of Margaux, grabbing it by the neck, and I wished I could ignore this, but she was gesticulating and waving it around and even shaking it as she spoke, and deep inside I groaned and was offended, watching her, yes, I'd have given anything just then if only she'd had some inkling that she was holding much more than a bottle of wine, much more than a very grand cru—if only she had realized that wrapped inside that tissue paper was something like my soul or, in any case, the very best I had to offer, and the final evidence of whatever had been invited mysteriously into our lives to alter both of their trajectories; but no, she gesticulated away thoughtlessly, disrespectfully, and I felt as though it were me she was swinging around in the air, all over again, without a word, without the slightest explanation, and in the end we'd never stood a chance—no man and woman ever did, and I didn't want to know or think about it anymore; she'd floored me, we were still in Round One of the party, and I was already down, as they say, for the count, and I distinctly felt some part of me detach itself, float across the room, and disappear out the bay window, and for whole seconds, all I could do was let my gaze wander over the people who revolved and surged around us, pausing now on one woman's tousled hair, now on the flame of a lighter, now on a petit toast sitting half-eaten in a saucer, and under the chair the stuffed cat was pouncing forever in vain, and the man in the panama hat had gone off someplace else, and finally I looked at her again and she was speaking to me through a sort of fog, and her shoulders were bare, and under her dress her small breasts were asserting themselves, and I had no business being there, I should never have come, and my whole life was going to be a horrific lipogram in which she, as the missing character, would never appear.

Maybe there was no more to say than what our eyes had already absorbed, and by now we had both fallen silent, unable to find the words that could take us back in time and space; then all of a sudden she stopped a woman going by and announced, in a mock-triumphant voice, "Sophie: your mystery guest." At this the woman turned to me, and her eyes were full of laughter and a lock of hair was plastered to her forehead and she looked excited, like a little girl who didn't know which way to turn, and in the moment nothing could have been more inaccessible and strange and finally intolerable as this enthusiasm of hers, this euphoria, it was more than I could face, and I tried to greet her with a stare that was inscrutable and chilly, because I certainly had no intention of playing a well-mannered mystery guest, no, from the beginning I'd sworn that I would preserve my dignity and cede nothing to a joke that, from my point of view and in my condition, had no chance of making me laugh, as if what we call society weren't already seeking at all times and in every way, including humor, to efface all individual personality, and so I had resolved not to be bullied or to put myself out, as they say; at the same time, in the moment I felt bovine and oafish and stupid and flushed, and in order not to just stand there mute, and end up blurting something idiotic anyway, I said "Happy birthday!" and she thanked me as she took the 1964 Margaux in her arms, and I hoped she would tear off the tissue paper then and there and show the world what I had done and go into ecstasies over my gift; but instead, she waved to someone across the room who must have just walked in, and then she turned around and considered me and asked in a joking way who I was, and she seemed to really want to know, because she was watching me closely, alertly, as if something inside had pricked up its ears, and I was grasping for something to say, to no great effect, and I felt more and more ridiculous and even guilty, as if I were somehow in the wrong, and finally I replied in a dry, pinched voice that I was, for the moment, an expert in the cruelties of existence, and I looked at her defiantly, I wanted to defy her, and if I looked like an idiot, so what? She didn't seem at all put out by my attitude, or annoyed, on the contrary, she kept staring and smiling, with a twinkle in her eye, and in fact I seemed to have amused her, and even intrigued her, and by chance our eyes met, and for a split second there was a spark, which quickly died away, and she was about to say something when an arm was thrown around her, and a woman with bloodred lipstick was shouting practically into her ear that they needed her in the kitchen right away; there'd been some disaster involving the oysters or whatever it was, and she looked apologetic and gave me a glance that could have meant lots of things or nothing at all as she let herself be dragged away toward the kitchen. Suddenly I realized that she was disappearing with the Margaux, and I almost shouted and ran after her, it was my wine, no one was going to help themselves to my wine, absolutely not! At my side, the person to whom I had everything to prove in that one night was just standing there, and I feverishly explained that I had brought a grand cru and that I was hoping we might share a toast, that's right, a toast, and even a toast "to love," as they say, and that was when she informed me that her friend never opened her birthday presents, and in the moment I tried to not believe what she was saying, but it was impossible. The error constituted by my presence at this party could only go so far. There had to be a limit. She must have said that to tease me, and to scare me, and to obliterate whatever was left of my authentic self; but she was serious, and she explained that for years Sophie had preserved all her birthday presents, unopened, in display cases and taken pictures of them afterward with the idea of maybe turning them someday into a show, or else a book, she wasn't sure which, in any case it had become a kind of ritual, and she really ought to have warned me when she called, but it didn't occur to her, and why would it, and why worry, after all it was only a bottle of wine, and I nodded and looked straight ahead and saw nothing except the wall, which had never stopped building itself around me and now seemed almost finished, and I couldn't stop nodding like one of those plastic dogs in the back of a car, and I thought no one would ever know the lengths to which I had gone, and that it had all been useless, it had all been for nothing, and what did I care if it helped the cause of modern art, I could give a shit, as they say, in fact I could give two shits, and I wanted to explode with laughter and blow out my jaw and my teeth and eyes and bones, and in the end what I wanted was to explode, just explode, and never be spoken of again.

I stepped into the garden to get some air, and the cold did me good; for a while I just stood there filling my lungs and puffing out steam and looking up at the stars. Way up there, the little probe *Ulysses* must have been moving at thousands of kilometers per second and making its way across the solar system, and even at this speed it would take years to reach the Sun, and I thought that in the end it was a kind of mystery guest in the galaxy who never gave up but faced perils considerably more daunting than anything in my way. Looking back through the bay window, I tried to spot her again, and she was talking to the man who'd made her laugh at the beginning, and surely this must be the man with whom she now shared her life, since he was touching her arm in an unmistakable way. What did she want to show me by bringing me here? Her new life? Her happiness? Her unhappiness? I didn't understand, there was something missing, and I needed to know what it was, I'd gone too far, I couldn't leave now, no, I couldn't face the next few hours alone, with no company but the after-image of a cat frozen in midleap, this had to be avoided, and I resolutely pushed open the sliding door and found myself back in the hubbub and warmth of the party, and I wanted a drink, I wanted several drinks, and I headed for the table while also checking the hallway to make sure my coat was still there; I had a sudden fear that it might have been stolen, or evaporated, and I needed to make sure neither thing had happened, and this couldn't wait, nothing else mattered, and in the end we only dread what has already invisibly come to pass, and next to my coat the bouquet of white and red roses seemed to be beckoning, as if it wanted to speak, and it was the one thing I could be sure about, the only benevolent thing, at that entire party.

I had reassumed my observation post under the stairs and was downing one glass of champagne after another, wait-ing for some kind of rescue, waiting for the pink flamingo to quit standing on one leg, when a woman with compli-cated earrings that dangled almost to her shoulders walked up and lifted her glass in my direction, and I didn't have much to say and didn't feel like talking, but I couldn't leave her there in front of me like a puddle, so I asked who all these people were who were having so much fun, and she started pointing people out and naming names, and most were people I'd heard of, and some were even famous, and there were artists there and writers and intellectuals and journalists and even a preeminent matador, and I told her it was funny, but to me all these celebrities didn't *look* like celebrities, to me they looked more like hunks of bread floating briefly on the surface of a bowl of milk, and I got the feeling that I'd said the wrong thing, as they say, because she stiffened ever so slightly, and in a voice that was meant to be joking, she said maybe I ought to switch to milk while her earrings tinkled their disapproval, and I bowed my head in acquiescence and contrition, but at the same time it was too late, something had been launched from way down deep within me, and, with a momentum of its own, it tore from my mouth, and before I could stop, I was having her know that, like it or not, it seemed to me we had a problem on our hands, yes, these elites who did such great things and defended even greater things, they were all well and good, they were fine, but could she name me one celebrity in this whole room who could claim to be "over and above it all"* and actually mean it, and that was something I'd like to see, I would be curious to see that, and she might recall this expression from when we used to say it, not so long ago, and no wonder if it had fallen into disuse and had even totally disappeared from our vocabulary, yes, nowadays nobody said or could say

---

* Grégoire seems to be scrambling two idioms: "*en avoir marre*" (to have had quite enough) and "*par-dessus le marché*" (furthermore). The second phrase, taken literally and out of context, could also mean "above the market."

that he was over and above it all because now we had lost not only the expression but the very possibility of being over and above it all; no one could even dream of such a thing, and the desire could no longer be put into words, and I wasn't quite sure where I was going with this, but the point was, could we be sure that in any other world, besides this one, these people would be famous or even exist, and if not, then what was the point of all their works or their renown, and there was no need for her to give me that look, no, because if she actually wanted to know, in a place like this I felt like the man on the street who no one ever mentions except to say how wrong he is and how misguided he is and how worthless, and how he ought to keep his mouth shut and how, in the end, he's nothing but a mystery guest, merely tolerated at the table of life, and what did she think about that? Not much, evidently, and I was already regretting my tirade and having attacked her; she was here at this party for a reason, and she could hardly be expected to understand, and I was ashamed, and, at the same time, I was relieved, yes, I was ashamed for no discernible reason and relieved for no discernible reason, and after several long seconds during which she treated me to her profile and the swaying of her pendants, which she absentmindedly fingered, she turned back to me and, staring as if suddenly I'd become an enemy, a personal enemy, she asked whether by any chance I happened to have published a book or anything of the sort, and I felt myself blushing and admitted that I hadn't, and her face relaxed and she smiled a little, as if everything had just been clarified, as if everything had been tidied up, as if no more need be said, now she understood where these words of mine were coming from, and the insignificance of my position could only signify the insignificance of anything I said, and she said what I was already expecting her to say, that it was easy and cheap to criticize people who actually did things, just because they took risks and tried to get things done, and there were plenty of arguments I could have made, but deep down I thought she was right and I didn't say anything, and she very quickly said, in a loud, distinct voice, that she would rather talk to someone who had talent or manners, and I said I understood, giving a low bow as she turned on her heel, ears rattling, and from where I stood I lifted my glass in her direction, and I was furious with myself, but at least we weren't married; you have to remember that things could always be worse. Isn't that what they told me all through my childhood to keep me quiet? At that moment, nothing struck me as more absurd, and even toxic and lethal, than to remain a quiet little boy for all time, to be seen and not heard, as they say.

Why wasn't she coming to talk to me? Now she was chatting with some other couple and seemed to have forgotten all about me, and I'd had enough of her antics, and of everything else, and I had definitely had enough of standing there under my staircase, so in order to save face and give myself an attainable goal, for once, I decided to steer my way over to the bay window, where I would see the party from an untested angle, yes, maybe I would see things and my life and the world in a new light once I got there, the thought occurred to me, sometimes it doesn't take much, and anyway it was a step in the right direction, and at least I'd made a decision, which was good in itself. At the same time I was keeping an eye out for our hostess, because the last thing I wanted was to cross paths with her; I felt so incapable just then of stringing together a sentence that wasn't fraught with distress and indigence, yes, it would be better for everyone, including me, if I kept quiet for the time being, that was much to be preferred, and in the end I was rounding a pillar behind which stood the man with the panama hat, and I hadn't seen him there, and he turned and fixed me with his very blue eyes, they were infinitely pale, and his face was strangely smooth and featureless, and at the same time gaunt, and he held out his hand, and in a soft, inaudible voice he said hello, and I took his hand and his hand was like his voice, and I smiled in the friendliest way I knew how, as if there were something about him that I was afraid of hurting, something vulnerable and even crying out for some kind of help, and I was about to withdraw my hand, but instead of letting go, he squeezed and held on, and what was going on? All at once he staggered and flew backward as if he were having some kind of paroxysm or fainting spell or as if something, I couldn't tell what, had suddenly overcome him, had liquefied him right there on his feet, and I saw him fading, and he wasn't struggling, on the contrary, he seemed to be letting himself go, and I thought he was going to collapse right there in front of me, and I panicked at the thought that he was having a seizure, and now I was the one who wouldn't let go of his hand, and I wanted to keep him from falling, no, please, anything but that, but it was all happening too fast and he was falling apart, right then and there, and I had to do something when my eyes met his and I realized this was no seizure, no, I'd seen this kind of look before, and something in me turned to rock, and I bore his desire without batting an eye, and he must have known that he had lost me, for he closed his eyes as if savoring some last regret, then slowly he opened them, and I asked in my harshest, most sarcastic voice whether he was feeling any better; but he paid no attention, and under his breath I heard him sigh "You are very beautiful," and I nodded and gritted my teeth, and I let go of his hand, and this time he let me go; the wave had passed, and once again his eyes were fathomless and tearful but now with something nasty and avid about them, and taking no more notice of me he walked off, with a limp, and I watched him go with growing disgust, fear, and humiliation. The whole scene couldn't have taken more than a couple of seconds, and no one had seen anything, and later I learned that he was Hervé Guibert, and he was the first writer I'd ever met in the flesh, as they say, and why bother having read all those books if it all came down to that, I moaned, and for a long time I'd been feeling spat on, and now I was sure of it, yes, nothing healthy was going to emerge from this accumulation of events, nor would I come out a better or more peaceful person, but instead I would come out diminished, and uglier, and vain and artistic and French and refuted once and for all, from head to toe.

•

But later in the party a slight woman with dark hair who must once have been very pretty, and still was, told me that she crossed the Montparnasse Cemetery on her way home every afternoon, and that every afternoon she made a detour to steal any flowers that had been left on the grave of Pierre Laval, and she would take them home with her and her house was perpetually full of flowers, as if by a miracle, and in any case it was remarkable enough, and in her words no flower deserved to die on such a grave, and it had become a kind of mission for her to save them, and her eyes glittered with malice, and I excused myself to make a phone call, and she pointed me to the right, and then I called the one who loved me despite my turtleneck undershirts, I'd promised I would call to reassure her, and I told her everything was going great, no need to worry, I was holding up fine and was heading home soon and would tell her all about it tomorrow and was thinking of her with lots of love, and at that moment this was truer than it had ever been before. I watched a young woman walk by in an orange bolero; I'd been struck by the sight of her several times before, despite everything that was cluttering up and twisting my mind, or maybe that was why, and I didn't know what I wanted from her, maybe just to hear her voice or speak to her, or to come up behind her and slip my hands under her bolero and feel her skin and englobe her breasts with my hands and caress and fondle them, without her protesting or being aroused or even surprised, on the contrary, she would close her eyes and let sensation take over, and everything would be simple and clear and luminous and orange, and wasn't I a guest of all the mysteries?

She was doing psych, as she put it, and while we stood there in the kitchen I kept her talking for as long as I could to prolong the presence of the line of her lips and the delicacy of her wrists and of her neck, which seemed to call out for strangulation, and I didn't quite follow every twist and turn of the conversation, but she'd just been describing the Lashley experiment, and I didn't know what that was, and she was explaining how they took rats and trained them to feed from a green trough and gave them an electric shock if they tried to eat out of a red trough, and the rats became neurotic, and so far so good, and I saw what she meant; but then they took away the green trough and now the rats had only the red trough to eat from, even though they knew they'd get electrocuted if they went near it, and you can imagine the conflict, she told me, her eyes shining; I certainly could, and in the end the rats go crazy: they start turning around in circles for hours on end or they become violent and aggressive for no apparent reason, and some devour their own extremities or throw themselves against the glass until they lose consciousness, and after several hours most of them end up immobile and prostrate and obsessive, so that they could be arranged into any pose, even the weirdest and most uncomfortable, without eliciting any reaction whatsoever. I finished my champagne in one gulp and told her that, in my opinion, for many of us, perhaps for all of us, the green trough had already been taken away, just look around and you'll see weird and obsessive poses everywhere and at all times, just look at the evening news, look at the incredibly obsessive way it reported all the things that had taken place in their own obsessive and incredible ways, and the unwelcome thought crossed my mind that my own way of being and doing—whatever it was I did, and even of writing—was no less weird or obsessive, and I fell into a kind of panic; all at once I broke out in a sweat and my turtleneck undershirt was choking me and sticking to my skin, and I spun around feverishly looking for a way out, there had to be a way out or else I couldn't take it, but I didn't see one and there wasn't one and I looked at her, and I could see her wondering what was the matter, and quickly I visualized her lips, her wrists, her neck, her bolero, and at once something expanded within me, and air and blood and life flowed in again, and in a stronger and even cheerful voice that betrayed nothing of my little tour of the abyss, I told her that it was a stroke of luck that she should be wearing an orange bolero and not a red one, yes, she could never imagine how lucky it was just then, it left some room for hope, and I wasn't thinking about her and me, despite what she must have thought since she gave a tight smile of mock indignation, and I didn't want to monopolize her, and it had been a pleasure to make her acquaintance, and she had taught me something and opened my eyes, and this was enough in itself.

•

The whole night all we'd done was cross paths and play a kind of careful hide-and-seek, and she hadn't once come up to me with any intention of referring to the past, much less of saying "I'm sorry," not even a simple *I'm sorry*, though that would have been enough, yes, without either of us referring to the past, I would have understood, just an *I'm sorry*, and maybe she could have taken my hand for a brief instant and given it a squeeze, yes, I'd have been satisfied with a little squeeze of the fingers and wouldn't have asked for anything more than that; but no, she was steadfast, and perhaps she hadn't found the courage or the moment or the desire or whatever it might have been. It didn't matter now; it was too late and the party was over. Still, I had tried to slip a foot in the door that had been closed for so many years: we were standing next to the bay window, and she had just shown me some photos of her daughter when, with an air of detachment, as they say, I asked if she'd heard about Michel Leiris; she replied that she had heard that he had died but she'd never read him, was he good? I shrugged. It wasn't the time to talk about books. Far from it. There was, however, no doubt: the death of Michel Leiris had unleashed nothing, the news of his death hadn't chimed in any way with her own disappearance, nor had it moved her to call me as I had supposed, and this metaphor was something I'd made up on my own to create some depth and meaning in her call, and to lend it an impact on the universe like the one it had for me, and now it was definitely time to go, yes, I couldn't waste another second in this room, among these people, all at once I was afraid of doing something—I didn't want to know what—if things

GRÉGOIRE BOUILLIER

went on this way, being normal and innocent and insidious and perfect and, underneath it all, hopeless and fake, those were the words I was looking for, and life could go on, and so could I. If we never got an explanation, we weren't the only ones, and my coat was there where I'd left it and so not all was lost, and as I bent down to get it, I looked at my hands and turned them palms up, and I saw my life running through my fingers like a fine rain of sand, and I didn't mind in the least.

I grabbed my coat, which had remained balled up in its corner like a faithful sleeping dog, and unconsciously I happened to glance at the bouquet of white and red roses, and it was actually magnificent and even, in that time and place, unexpectedly beautiful, and despite myself I gave in to this vision and let myself be overcome; each flower seemed to have been placed in such a way that all were united by a tacit, spontaneous line, and the whole arrangement expressed a harmony that exalted no one flower in particular, and excluded none, yes, each rose seemed to blossom according to its own potential, and at the same time each took part in the composition of the whole, and I was reflecting that whomever had arranged those roses probably cherished certain utopian ideals and had tried to express them in a vase of water, perhaps not even by choice, when I felt her presence behind me. She must have seen that I was heading out, even making a dash, as they say, and taking French leave, as they say, and that I was the one about to leave without saying a word. I hadn't seen her approach but knew it was her and didn't move; I wanted to spend one last moment contemplating the comforting and frankly nostalgic ocean of white and red petals before I faced this immense defeat of ours, which I knew would never cease to haunt me once I passed through the sliding door. I wasn't in such a hurry anymore, and, playing for time to put off the moment when I would have to stand up and look at her and everything would be over, I said in a slightly choked voice, "It really is a beautiful bouquet, isn't it?" And I felt myself trying to cram our entire history into those thirteen syllables, as if I got to say the last word, as if there needed to be a last word, as if that were the right thing to do, and suddenly I knew I was putting on an act and playing myself and my own feelings, as if my only way out was to mime them and package them the right way, in accordance with all the reassuring rules of fiction, as if I had no existence outside this effort at falsification, no existence at all in what I actually felt, and no access to what I felt except through a preconceived, simplistic, pat, plausible, easy, and in the end, culturally specific idea, and this final, internalized denial of everything I was experiencing was the low point of the entire night, and it was too late: believability was all I had left, and I kept quiet, well aware that these few seconds of silence were creating a "painful intensity" between us and an "ineffable emotion" and that, in a situation like ours, this was exactly the thing to do: suspend time in order to make believe that something "beyond words" was taking place, something fraught with all the buried sadness in the world, and maybe in the end it was true, yes, even though I knew this silence was artificial and stagey and a total cliché, as they say, I gave in and let myself be engulfed and all at once, I felt moved and sincere and close to her, as I hadn't once felt this whole time since she'd called and I'd seen her again, yes, all at once our separation was working to bring us together and it was succeeding, in front of this bouquet and in the silence, and during these few altered seconds, everything became truly beautiful and harmonious and red and white and orange between us, and I wanted to believe, and just then I could feel us looking in the same direction, no doubt for the last time, and I felt that to end on that note, as they say, was enough. With my coat under my arm, I stood and looked to get one last image of her face, and her eyes were on the bouquet and without glancing away she said, barely moving her lips, that roses were the only flowers that she could bear to see cut, and with those words the contempt I had suffered by being there melted away.

It was her tone of voice. There was something ineffable and spontaneous about it, a sort of aura I didn't recognize, almost a presence, and it startled me, something in me stirred and came to life and paid attention, as if someone had poked me in the shoulder or pinched me, and now her voice sounded so unlike her, so weird, that I actually thought it was someone else, but I knew it was her; this feeling only lasted a split second, but it opened up an abyss before me and plunged me into a state of tingling disbelief that she seemed not even to notice, yes, I was watching her and her face gave me nothing, the moment had passed and seemed never to have happened, and she was giving me the same smooth, friendly, and finally impermeable gaze that had protected her through the entire party, and I no longer knew what to think except that I intuited, actually I knew, that this had been no meaningless remark, that on the contrary this little phrase of hers had a meaning and even a raison d'être; it sounded like a slip of the tongue, there is no other way to say it, and right away I sensed that she had sent me a kind of message and a sign from deep within, yes, at the most unexpected and least predictable moment, she had somehow betrayed herself and let something escape, and it had reached me and made itself plain, and addressed me even though I'd lost hope, as if this time she couldn't quite let me go without a word, without the slightest explanation, yes something in her finally rebelled, and for all her defenses and silences and her unalterable rigidity and certainly her guilt, she had tried and managed to tell me this one thing that, obscurely and, so to speak, unconsciously, she had been planning to tell me from the very moment she picked up the phone to invite me to this fateful party, and only at the last moment had she found the strength and the opportunity to loosen the vice and stretch out her hand and wave her handkerchief from her tower, and it had to do with "cut roses" and "the only thing she could bear to see," and I had no idea what this meant, but I knew, I just knew, that she was letting me in on a secret, and wasn't this just the kind of thing I'd hoped for when I came? Five minutes later I was on the street, having kissed her goodbye in a perfectly normal way, leaving as if we'd said it all and turned the page, as they say, and I knew we had.

I headed home through unfamiliar streets. I'd never have found a taxi at that hour in that neighborhood, and anyway I wanted to walk and be by myself and take my time and move at my own pace, not the speed of a car or public transit, no, just then I needed to feel, physically and mentally and personally, all the distance between myself and home, and for once I didn't want to be reassured, as I sped along, that nothing happens as one goes from one place to another, as if every place was equal and finally one and the same, in fact the one and only monotonous place one never leaves, and in the cold I congratulated myself for the first time on having worn a turtleneck undershirt even as I thought, and I never stopped thinking, about that little phrase of hers, which was creeping and crawling and worming around and digging its tunnels inside me as I looked back on the party and recapitulated its various events, which now struck me as laughable and harmless and, in any case, they hadn't been awful or insurmountable—not the way I'd dreaded, and how could I have imagined that I would arrive at this party to find the world and all its powers and stratagems ranged against me, as they say, or that everyone was going to see all my failings and impotence and insignificance? What a baby I was. When you got right down to it, I was ludicrous, I deserved a good spanking, I deserved to be slapped, and I'd rather not think of it ever again. So roses were the only flowers she could bear to see cut? What was she talking about? Certain conjectures sprang automatically to mind, and no doubt one could draw all sorts of conclusions about women in general and her in particular from the words "roses" and "cut," but this didn't get me very far, and anyway it was beside the point. I knew this had to do with something else, I was sure of it, yes, it was in my presence that the tiny shift had taken place in her, and her little phrase was meant for me, and the same way I knew I hadn't been dreaming I also knew that she had offered me the key to her silence for all those years, and that this key could only fit and turn in the lock of our shared history, this much was clear as day; her little phrase wouldn't open anything at all in any other story but ours, and in this case any self-centered interpretation, focused on its own interpretive powers, wouldn't be worth a hill of beans, as they say, and maybe that was true in every case. None of which helped to decipher the message that she had transmitted and, as it were, deposited into my hands, and I was far from doing so—no doubt as far as I was from home, for I could turn those words in every direction and arrange and rearrange them and move them this way and that and I got nowhere and couldn't find any way out, so that the whole party would turn out to have been an unspeakable farce, and soon no doubt I would have persuaded myself that it had all been in my head, and that she hadn't actually been trying to tell me anything, and all because I remained deaf to the mysterious invitation that she had thrown me like a lifesaver, and to my right a street sign was pointing the way to Paris, and

I sighed with relief to see that I hadn't lost my way and that in fact I was near someplace I knew.

In an odd way, it seemed to me that I had already lived through this scene, or no, I hadn't lived through it, not exactly, it was more like the powerful scent of a forest after a rainstorm flooding a sealed room in an apartment. The thought drifted down over me like a kind of fog, and I found myself smiling; it was so crazy and came so completely out of nowhere, and no doubt physical and nervous exhaustion had something to do with it, because I certainly was exhausted, and, as I walked along, I saw a bedroom in perfect detail, a bedroom assailed by the effluvia of wood and wet leaves, and the air was cool and vaguely fetid, and the room was awash in the perfectly recognizable odor of acorns and moss and mushrooms even as I saw before me a table, chairs, a bed, a richly patterned rug, a painted ceiling, shelves lined with books, and, unless we'd been lied to for centuries, these surroundings could hardly be called a forest, much less a forest after a rainstorm, or even a forest without the rain, yes, it was simple and disorienting at the same time, and this vision filled me with happiness, with irrational joy, like a punch line: my eyes were completely at odds with my sense of smell, or vice versa, and so which sense was telling the truth and which was fooling the other? The question seemed all the more pressing since in fact I have no sense of smell, and . . . Mrs. Dalloway! Just like that, the name flashed before my eyes, and an incredible fever shot through my veins and the night began to dance around me, and it couldn't be, it made no sense. What was the Virginia Woolf novel doing here? And what would occur to me next? But I felt myself gripped by a great foreboding, as if lifted bodily from the earth and thrown into the air, and I got goose bumps, as they say, and my legs grew so weak that they started to wobble, and how could I be wrong when my blood was jubilating in my veins? A feeling like this couldn't lie, yes, her little phrase had some connection to *Mrs. Dalloway*, the sudden revelation had me seeing stars, and with every step I took, it became a more and more prodigious certainty, for now everything followed, the mere mention of the name made everything clear. With one push, it threw open a hidden door and out came a swirling, jostling, surging blizzard of words, and suddenly I recalled there was something in the book about red and white roses and a bouquet, which functioned somehow in the plot, I couldn't remember how, and it had to do with a reunion at a fancy party, yes, a woman reconnected with the great love of her youth during a big reception, and I couldn't remember his name, but she was the one who invited him—I was pretty sure she was the one—and they reconnected after years of separation and I couldn't remember how the book ended, and that wasn't all, there was something else, yes, now I remembered that she loved Virginia Woolf and that *Mrs. Dalloway* was one of her favorite books, maybe her very favorite at the time. She once read me several passages out loud and, in any case, I could clearly remember how moved she was when she closed the book, and it must have been when we were first in love, and never, as far as I knew, had any book affected her that way, it wasn't even really her kind of thing, no, in those days she usually went around with big thick history books or multigenerational sagas and, in any case, I had promised to read this book she adored, and in the end, I didn't read it until years later, and actually it was a while after she'd left, and in the moment I didn't find it as amazing as all that; it wasn't really my kind of thing, either. In those days I preferred Joyce's *Ulysses*, which Woolf tried to take further in her own way, and it was crazy: every second revealed some new source of excitement, and everything now took on an unexpected, stunning new meaning, and the pieces of this puzzle of mine were magically coming together, and it felt like an explosion in my head as thousands of chips came clattering down, and I actually heard them clattering down in a cascade like coins in a slot machine, saying this was my lucky day, and I'd won the jackpot, and in the end life was an exuberant adventure. I was practically running down the street to get home, yes, I couldn't wait to find out whether I'd got it right or whether this was simply the ultimate delusion of my fevered brain, and I took the stairs four by four and dashed to the bookshelf without even taking off my coat to look for Woolf's book, but I couldn't find it and I thought I'd lose my mind. For half a second this was no joke, and I had to tear all the books off the shelves before I finally found the little gray book that held within it all my hopes, and in a kind of delirium I plunged into the story of Clarissa Dalloway and Peter Walsh, and there it was on page 140: "But she loved her roses . . . the only flowers she could bear to see cut."

The book couldn't have been more explicit, and by the time I closed it, I had found my words and my explanation, yes, here were a thousand sentences that answered all those long-unanswered questions, and all the answers to the questions I'd never thought to ask, and finally I knew why she'd called me to invite me to that party, and I knew why she'd been silent ever since she left, and maybe even what made her leave in the first place. Because the entire book made it clear that it wasn't her who called to invite me to that party, it was Mrs. Dalloway, or rather the spirit of Mrs. Dalloway, which had possessed her just as the spirit of *Ulysses* stuck with me after she left, starting then, yes, I wasn't the only one who had experienced such bizarre sublimations, or even total metamorphoses; it happened to other people too, starting with her, and it was both scary and amazing, and it all fit together too neatly not to be true, and, in any case, I wasn't about to turn up my nose at any justification for what had been, from the time she left until that party, a continual riddle and torment to me, not even if the reality of the thing, as they say, was something else entirely, not even if my judgment and memories were wrong, not even if they were tainted by my sense of her now. Who owned my reality? I was a human being, too, in my way, and when I looked at these events through the lens of Woolf's novel, I was finally able to believe, and to hope, that they'd happened for a reason, and that this reason was accessible to me, yes, all of a sudden they no longer struck me as absurd and chaotic and disastrous, but rather as logical and inspired and lifesaving, as I saw one page after another transposed into reality and saw how wonderfully, given the means at her disposal and how little she had to work with, she had tailored Woolf's novel to her own life and, unbeknownst to her or anyone else, had followed the program she glimpsed there—not just in outline, but down to the letter—with all the emotions and sensations that she loved to feel and that, I was now convinced, she had obscurely dreamed of making her own, as if the best and deepest part of her wanted to live, and even insisted on living, by feelings other than fear, to which the world seems ever more determined to shrink us down, one by one. The roses, the reunion, the party: it was all right here, in black-and-white, and a crowd of details that I remembered from her life leapt out at me, as they say, and they all pointed to Clarissa Dalloway and testified to a love that was glorious and beyond reproach and unique, so that Clarissa Dalloway lingered across time and space like a scent that she had secretly made into an essence of her own, until there was no way to reach her except through that atmosphere, and I thought with a kind of fright and joy that if she left me without a word, without the slightest explanation, it might be because, from the very beginning, she had nursed the unspeakable plan of our meeting years later in order to play out this scene, with her as Clarissa Dalloway, in which she was reunited, over the course of a party, with the man she loved in her youth, and in the end hadn't everything happened to let this occur in real life? And if so, what did real life actually mean? For hadn't she arranged it so that someday I too would cry out "Clarissa! Clarissa!" although "she never came back" and "he never saw her again"? And did she really think I wouldn't recognize her in this woman who "never lounged in any sense of the word," who was "straight as a dart, a little rigid in fact" and, at the same time "pure-hearted," terrified of death and capable of proclaiming that "what she liked was simply life"? Yes, it was a spitting image of her, and the more I thought, the more it seemed to me that she had found, in the man who became the father of her daughter, a real Richard Dalloway too: "grey, dogged, dapper, clean," who, from everything I'd heard, could be described as "pertinacious and dogged, having championed the downtrodden and followed his instincts," and when I remembered how they looked together I could quite easily imagine him saying "it was a miracle that he should have married Clarissa," and nothing was missing, not even his daughter with the "Chinese eyes in a pale face; an oriental mystery," whose photo she'd shown me next to the bay window, yes, even the smallest detail of her life suddenly revealed a meaning that owed nothing to chance but owed everything to her desire to be purged of the formless and the mediocre, so that she might rise to the condition of the novelistic, and, in any case, that's what I believed and wanted to believe and, at the end of the day, it was my own face that I discovered through her eyes in the character of Peter Walsh.

So she'd left without a word, without the slightest explanation, so what? It didn't matter anymore. I was over it. Finally. But could this really be? I could hardly believe it myself, and yet I felt no more bitterness; all my rancor and despair had disappeared and seemed to have vanished as if by magic, or rather had been transmuted and transformed into a sort of gratitude and tenderness and even admiration for her and her achievement, yes now I knew and understood how highly she valued her existence, and how I came to pay the price, as they say, yes, quite apart from any cruelty I suddenly saw and acknowledged that all she'd ever wanted was to "save that part of life, the only precious part, this center, this ravishment that men let slip away, this prodigious joy that could be ours," as it said in the publisher's blurb, and, at any rate, amid all the powers that sway us and try to tell us what to do, she had managed to rebel and to endure without choking off the lifeline that I say matters most, matters more than everything else, and, in the end, she chose me to hear her secret, and no doubt she had waited until the last possible moment because the novel ends at the very end of the party, and at the very moment when Peter Walsh gets ready to go, and that was enough for me, I had my explanation, and it was worthy of her and me, and it sold for twelve francs fifty and it was Sunday, October 14, 1990, and once again everything was happening on a Sunday: without any premeditation, at the same time of day that I'd received the call that tore me from my sleep two weeks before, I called the one who loved me despite my turtleneck undershirts, knowing that my life was now in her delicate small hands, yes, once again I could look forward to a new chapter of my life, since I'd finally turned the page, as they say, and no doubt this chapter would be just as obscure and confusing as the others, no doubt the pages would share a common grain between the

lines, but this chapter would lend our gestures and deeds a
style all its own, a style to vouch that things were actually
taking place, and I knew this as a happy certainty in my
veins, and on the other end of the line, her voice already felt
like a hug, fertile with hope, and even as I was reporting all
the little misadventures I'd had at the party, I looked out
the window and saw the sky and the roofs and the Sunday
gray of the universe and I felt that I too could acquire what
Woolf called "the power of taking hold of experience, of
turning it round, slowly, in the light," and I wanted that
power badly, and the next day the radio announced that
Delphine Seyrig had died, and in my heart I knew it had
happened the day before, and not at Marienbad.

It sounds like no big thing, but that was the day I bought
a light bulb to replace the one in the bathroom. For I
don't know how many weeks, maybe months, the bulb had
been burned out, and yet I'd never changed it or made the
slightest move in that direction; despite the inconvenience
and even the absurdity of washing every morning in the
dark and dealing with the faucets without being able to see
them or compose my face in the mirror, I had let this go
on until I'd become totally used to it, though the one who
loved me despite my turtleneck undershirts complained
whenever she stayed over, and in the mornings I'd hear
her raving and complaining and accusing me of being lazy
and absentminded and, later, of being self-absorbed and
of never thinking about her needs and of not having any
respect for her and, why not just say it, of not loving her,

because it's not as if we were living in Peru, she would say, anyone could just go out and buy a light bulb, and it was the least I could do, and if I thought she was going to take care of it, forget it, because she wasn't, and the whole thing was grotesque, she would end up grumbling, though I'd put my arms around her and said it was no more absurd than all the other broken things in this world, and as she pushed me away, half laughing, half furious at my evasion, she replied that this was no reason to add to the pile, and I nodded and promised that the light bulb would be changed that very day, and for months I didn't lift a finger, as they say; and all of a sudden it occurred to me to buy a light bulb; I even felt an urge to buy one, as if it were the most natural thing in the world, and in less time than it takes to write the words, I had screwed in a magnificent 60-watt krypton over the bathroom mirror, and I could already imagine her satisfaction when she found that I'd finally kept my word as I jiggled the used-up bulb to hear the little sound of the filament, and only then did I realize that it was really and truly dead, and at that moment I wasn't thinking about some light bulb, no, all at once I understood that I was able to replace this bulb because the light had come back on in some dark recess of my being, and so now it made sense that there should be light in the bathroom, and what was the point of living if all we did was go around conforming to the will of inanimate objects? Changing a bulb, why? To make a bathroom happy? I'd been right not to change that bulb; I had been right to *refuse* to change it, in spite of everything, since changing it would have meant nothing to me, no, there was nothing

silly about my stubbornness, and that's what I had learned
from the party, and it occurred to me that the whole thing
might never have taken place except to achieve the shining
and cosmic, or at least incontestable, result of my man-
aging to change a miserable bulb in the bathroom, and I
almost laughed at my reflection in the mirror, and in the
face of a world so bent on problem-solving that it never
bothers to ask what the problems mean to us, or ought to
mean. And then I thought of how she herself owned an
electric kettle that shocked her every third time she turned
it on and how every time it happened she would yell and
jump and swear she was going to throw it away as soon as
we'd finished breakfast and how she never did, claiming
some obscure sentimental attachment, and now I understood that she was holding on, not to the kettle itself, but
to the fact of its not working, which changed everything
and shed all sorts of new light on her and maybe on everything that ever went wrong on the planet, and I thought
that giving her a new kettle, as I'd been planning to do for
some time now, was the very last thing to do and the most
inappropriate and the least helpful when it came to taking
hold of experience and turning it slowly in the light, no,
a new kettle would only make things worse and alienate
her further from herself, I thought, and when she arrived
at my house in her ravishing little navy blue dress with
the white polka dots, whose effect on me she knew, I told
her all the insane thoughts that had been going through
my head while I'd been waiting, and we were standing in
the bathroom, which now was lit up like Versailles, and
she looked at me with tenderness and amusement, and I

took her small hands in mine, and she leaned in to kiss me, and this kiss went on for years and swept away all the turtleneck undershirts on Earth and all the desperations and despairs that they had held tucked away inside since their invention.

Finally I could breathe. Space and time came alive for me and seemed endless, and in her arms the nights were full of sun, and for what may have been the first time with a woman, I felt utterly capable and at my best, and so it was that four years later we had a little girl—this was in December 1994, and what little I know about this I only learned much later, but that same year, that month, the probe *Ulysses* finally reached the Sun after having traveled millions of kilometers from Earth, and on that same day in October of 1990 my life started over and things between us came unstuck, so to speak, and wasn't that something? Wasn't it a wonder of astronomical proportions? Barring any accident, *Ulysses* would keep going, according to a trajectory planned and calculated from Earth, on an immense space voyage that would bring it back close to the sun in 2001, and at the time I had no way of knowing what was happening overhead. I hadn't the slightest idea or even any suspicion, but over those same years I too had the feeling that I was moving away from the light and plunging ineluctably into the darkness and emptiness once she left me, soon after she'd given birth and, so to speak, accomplished her mission with me, no, in the end things didn't work out, and this time I had my hands so full of words and explanations they kept me wide awake and didn't give me so much as an afternoon of sleep, and I thought opportunity would never come knocking again, or call on the phone, no, it never comes in the same form twice, I thought, and I had to give up waiting; I wouldn't get another mysterious invitation to persevere and fight on and live, but I was wrong: one night when we'd drunk a lot of beer by the light of an immense hanging candelabra, the publisher who would soon be mine contracted me to finish a text in which I told, not the story of my life, which held as little interest as anyone else's, but what my life had told me and what I thought I had grasped of its language, and finally a book came out in 2001, and it wasn't as if I'd timed it this way on purpose. Incredible as it may seem, and incredible as it seems to me, I had finally accomplished, in the same amount of time as a tiny little probe, a slow and vast orbit across the space that constituted my own life story, and for the first time I felt as though I were approaching, in words, a sun I could call my own, and by this time Michel Leiris had been dead twelve years, and it had been more than fifteen years since he had written that "literary activity, in its specific aspect as a mental discipline, cannot have any other justification than to illuminate certain matters for oneself at the same time as one makes them communicable to others, and that one of the highest goals . . . is to restore by means of words certain intense states, concretely experienced and become significant, to be thus put into words," and that, I told myself, is where everyone ought to start.

IV

The whole thing might have ended there and, normally, it should have. But at a party to which I'd been brought by "the Lyonnaise," my private name for a very young woman whose company was brightening certain hours of my days, I was told that someone wished to speak to me and even insisted on meeting me and congratulating me on my book, and it was a woman, she was waiting at the bar, and it was Sophie Calle. At first I didn't quite put it all together; but as I crossed the room I felt a wave of excitement and even a sort of thrill at the prospect of seeing this person in whose home my life had, in a sense, turned around ten years before and without whose intervention none of it would have happened, yes, all at once the business of being a mystery guest came rushing back and, with it, an undiminished sense of the miraculous, a sense, I suddenly realized, that I had lost and forgotten over all these years under a thousand other memories, and as I threaded my way through small groups of guests toward the bar, I felt as if I was reconnecting with a high point in my past and reliving it, and I almost expected everything to start all over again. It was so strange and even uncanny to see her again at exactly the same kind of party, as if all the years and lives in the meantime, all the births and deaths had never really taken place, as if now that she'd sorted out the problem in the kitchen with the oysters we'd get a chance to talk. At the same time I had no clear memory of what she looked like, and I wouldn't

GRÉGOIRE BOUILLIER

have been able to pick her out on the street, and it was only
when I found myself standing right in front of her that I
was struck all over again—despite her glasses with their
big, serious black frames, which I didn't remember her
wearing—by her frank, laughing look, and she still had a
lock of hair falling over her forehead, and she was wearing
a low-cut dress that showed off her breasts to great advantage, and I was very happy to see her again, I was absolutely
delighted, and I clasped her hand, and she said that she was
delighted, too, and she quickly turned the conversation to
the book I had written, and she spoke with great sincerity,
and the longer she spoke, the clearer it became, not only
that she didn't recognize me, but that my face didn't ring
a bell, as they say, she obviously didn't remember that I
had been one of her mystery guests, she hadn't a clue,
and I felt as though everything in the room was slowly
becoming unreal and wobbling and crumbling, and for a
second I gripped the stool underneath me with both hands
and dug my nails in under my thighs to convince myself
that everything wasn't about to vanish in a puff of smoke,
including me, and at the same time I kept smiling, and
I forced myself to concentrate on what she was saying,
and I went on nodding, as is my wont, keeping to myself
the horrific sensation of sliding slowly down the length of
my own body into a widening puddle on the floor. You're
right, I said, trying to pull it together, what's important is
not that one *say* everything but in the end that everything
be *said*, and the truly exciting thing, the dangerous thing,
is to confront not just what has happened, but what one
knows to have happened, and well, I don't want to sound

pretentious . . . and, as hoped, this oratorical sleight of hand won a smile, and her teeth were dazzling, and just then her entire face was spontaneous and open, and there was something luminous about her, and just like the first time, I felt a sort of spark leap between us, more than a spark, and it was the bouquet—in my head I told myself it was the bouquet and repeated that it was yet again, and always, and forever the bouquet and even this time a Big Bouquet, and for a split second it crossed my mind that perhaps my whole life had been no more than a bumbling inquiry into this expression, which didn't actually mean anything, yes, all at once it struck me as stupid and useless and incomprehensible, and point-blank I asked her if she knew the origin of the expression *"c'est le bouquet,"* I was sorry to cut her off, but there was something I needed to tell her, yes, in fact we had met once before, there was no reason she would remember, but I had been one of her mystery guests, really I had, maybe ten years before, and wasn't it funny, wasn't it something, and then I came out and summarized the story of how I had come to play the official stranger at her birthday, and we could easily figure out which year it was because Michel Leiris had just died and I met Hervé Guibert and so it had to be before he died, and she reflected that it must have been in 1990 because she left France later that year, and the whole time as I went on talking and adding details and laying my cards on the table, as they say, she never looked away, and she was gazing deep into my eyes, and I felt as though she was captivated and I could tell her anything, and I confessed that, at the time, I experienced the whole night as a sort of humiliation, especially when I found out that she took pictures of the presents without opening them, and at the word *humiliation* her gaze clouded over and a light went out, and she said she had absolutely no memory of me, she was sorry, in fact she was surprised, and I could see she thought I might have made the whole story up, and I said it was only natural that she'd have forgotten because I'd been a lousy mystery guest, in fact I'd made only a brief appearance at her party, and she was the one who, without knowing it, had played a huge and unexpected role in my life and in the end, I told her, I owe you a debt of gratitude,* and in a way you could even say that I am one of your works, and she pursed her lips to signify that this sort of flattery was wasted on her, that I could save it, and instantly I rejoiced, and I found her more and more adorable and worthy of something even beyond adoration, and to change the subject I asked whether I'd brought her a lucky year, in the end, and she told me that was the year she moved to the United States and married a man named Greg.

Obviously this had nothing to do with me, but still it was quite a coincidence, and in the moment I couldn't help thinking that she might associate my name with her husband's, and laughing I warned her that she'd better not amputate my "goire" as if I already knew that we'd see each other again, and speaking of her husband she asked whether I'd seen the film she'd made of their unlikely wedding in

---

* Literally, "*une fière chandelle*" (quite a candle).

Las Vegas, and I admitted that I had only heard of it, yes, after this mystery guest business and the Margaux I'd kept my distance from her work, and all these years I had purposely not kept up with her career and had even made a point of avoiding her name and had basically behaved as if nothing she might photograph or exhibit or write could tell me anything about her that I didn't already know all too well, and anyway contemporary art, as they say, did nothing for me, at any rate nothing good; the same was true of other media, and of course that just showed how little I knew, I added as I refilled our glasses of red wine, and if I'd wanted to provoke her I was wasting my time, because she clearly didn't mind—on the contrary, my attitude seemed to suit her just fine; she even seemed to like it, and all I knew was what a friend had told me, that in one scene she and her husband filmed each other playing some kind of game, Truth or Dare or something, and at one moment she made some gesture, I forget what, I think maybe she lowered the camera and stopped filming, and suddenly it was as if she had laid down her arms and proposed a truce, the way no one is ever brave enough to do, and she wasn't imposing terms the way we all do, in couples or elsewhere, and it was horrible, according to this friend of mine, who was having his own problems with his wife, because her husband refused to give it up, he kept filming and he clung to his camera and hid behind it, as if he couldn't or wouldn't or refused to see that she had tried to climb down from her tower and come out into the open and wave a white flag, and this friend told me that he understood and even sympathized with what was going through her husband's head, but in the moment he desperately wished her husband could at least try to not leave her in this position, to not leave himself in this position, and in the end things didn't go at all well with his wife, and he told me that it was the shortest and most tragic and in the end the most radical love scene he had ever seen in any movie, it was the first time someone had captured the impossible demand made by women and the impossible acquiescence of men and the curse that separates them, the familiar curse that hangs over us all like a kind of dismay and, I was sorry; I was babbling, and in any case I hadn't seen her film, and besides I didn't like movies in general, and she was lighting a cigarette and said she'd really like to meet this friend of mine, and now I saw her eyes in tears, I mean I saw tears in her eyes, I forget how you say it, and this emotion was completely unexpected and she wasn't trying to hide it or impose it on me; it was just there, like a sort of vast, naked, simple sadness, and all I could do was wait for it to pass, there was nothing to say just then, and that was all right, and she took a couple of drags of her cigarette, and drank her wine, then she looked up and gave me a dazzling smile that was, just then, like an invention she tore out of herself, and she asked brightly whether I was planning to write anything else, and I said an astrologer had predicted years before that one day I'd write a book and it would be a success and then I'd never write anything again.

•

She herself was doing a project with an astrologer and putting together a big show, and she was full of stories, each crazier, funnier, sadder, and more extravagant than the last—*extravagant* was her word. It felt like centuries since I'd spoken so naturally and freely with a woman, as if we were speaking the same language, and it was unfettered; that's the thing: this language was absolutely unfettered, and it seemed to have fed on so many defeats that we'd each experienced, endured, and overcome and turned into anecdotes, that all either of us had to do to feel alive was polish up the facets, and from time to time my gaze lingered on her shoulders and her breasts and her lips and she noticed and never stopped smiling, and there was something Talmudic in her smile, and I wanted to brush aside that annoying lock of hair, which reminded me uncomfortably of my turtleneck undershirts, so that I could finally see her forehead and let her face appear in the light and be itself, and she told me that I was obviously invited to her next birthday, when she'd be turning fifty. She said this with utter serenity, without any coyness or embarrassment, but I felt a pang, as if a tiny cloud had drifted across the sunlight that was shining there between us, fifty? Had she really said fifty? That couldn't be right, until that moment I hadn't given a thought to her age or noticed it, that was the thing, and it was nuts, she couldn't be fifty years old, what did she mean, fifty? I was forty-three and she seemed so buoyant and graceful, and in a certain way childlike, and I realized my trouble wasn't her age, it wasn't how old she was today and at this party, no, but what it suddenly meant for the future, that was frightening and unbearable and scandalous, yes, in five years she'd be fifty-five and then sixty, and that vision was hopeless and implacable as if, for the first time, I was glimpsing my own old age and was racing toward it, and even as I told her happily that I'd be delighted to attend, I felt myself trying to squeeze my eyes shut and not see or know any more about the cruelty of existence, and without having the actual words, I knew in the blink of an eye that another little phrase was about to avenge itself on the phrase that years before had opened such broad vistas and offered me the hope and innocence of the future on a platter, and just then time seemed to me the worst mystery guest of them all, and when I said goodbye a little while later, to leave with the woman who had brought me to the party, I kissed her softly on the lips as if this kiss in itself could efface all the injustice and ignominy that lie ahead of us, and lie in wait.

Three days later she called me. Something extravagant had happened, she said, something completely insane, something that had never happened before, she still couldn't believe it and was laughing to herself on the other end of the line, and it had to be some kind of sign, and had she caught me at a bad moment? My story about having been the mystery guest had intrigued her, and she'd gone to the book where she listed all the birthday presents she'd been given over the years, looking to see whether she could find that bottle of Margaux, and she couldn't find any trace of it, not in the chapter devoted to 1990 or anywhere else. I was about to swear that I'd been telling the truth, and this couldn't be, and when was it ever going to end?, when she quickly told me that, in a spirit of due diligence, she had gone down into the basement where she stored her works, and I wasn't going to believe this, it was extravagant, she had rummaged around all over, really she'd wasted hours hunting up and down when, take it from her, she had plenty of other things to do. In any case, it seemed impossible that I was lying, and at very least she wanted to have a clean conscience, and I already knew what she was about to say, and sure enough on a top shelf, way high up, she had found a bottle of wine wrapped in tissue paper, and it was a 1964 Margaux and could only be my bottle, and she'd found it! With great ceremony, she read the label over the phone: *"Grand cru classé—Château du Tertre—1964—Appellation Margaux contrôlée—mis en bouteilles au château—propriétaire,"* and what could I say except that it was, indeed, extravagant and, at the same time, it had all happened so long ago that I didn't know what I felt or whether this bottle still meant anything to me; but it was enough, and she couldn't get over the thought that this bottle should have spent all those years in the dark on one of her shelves when she was so extremely organized and scrupulous, and I couldn't tell anyone, I had to swear secrecy, and I swore, but this was the only time she'd ever been caught out in her work, and after all she did have an excuse, really she did, because there was no name on the bottle to indicate who might have brought it, and since she didn't know me, she had assumed that the mystery guest had left one of two IOUs that she had found the day after the party, and since no one had ever come to honor them, she had every reason to suppose that I must have been the source of one or the other, and besides that was what she had written in her book, and she was going to send me a copy right away bearing the necessary correction, and she was enchanted by the adventure of the thing, and her voice was trembling with excitement on the other end of the line, and she couldn't stop saying how extravagant it was, and I could hear her walking around and never standing in one place, since her heels were echoing and clacking on what must have been tile, and she was in fact in the kitchen and like a crazy person was trying to figure out where to put the bottle so she could keep it out of the sunlight and look at it at the same time, and I absolutely had to come over and see it right away; suddenly she found the responsibility overwhelming, and in the taxi back to where everything had started eleven years before, the driver didn't tell me any story, and he was disagreeable even, while on the radio a journalist, as they say, devoted a feature to the writer-director of the movie *Die Hard*, who had recently been hired by the US government so that he could help the military develop strategic scenarios and, if I understood correctly, so that fiction might come to the aid and the service and the rescue of reality, as if reality weren't always already a fiction, and as I looked out the window at the road I had already traveled, I thought of all the events that had taken place all over the world, and all the beings and things, and of my wayward and basically lucky life, and we had arrived, and paying the fare in a currency that was no longer the same as before, I wondered what book might be lying on her bedside table, and at that moment I was eager to find out.

·

A year later I was in Erquy, on my way to Plurien, Côtes-d'Armor. It was unusually mild for early February, and I was hunting for seashells on the deserted beach and reflecting on this story of the mystery guest, which I had decided to tell, yes, I wanted to prove the astrologer wrong, and all the stars, and why mince words: at the very same moment that I wrote "It was the day Michel Leiris died," but unbeknownst to me, the directors of NASA and the European Space Agency were deciding to extend the mission of the space probe *Ulysses* until 2008, yes, although the mission was set to end in February 2004, after fourteen years of good and faithful service and two successful rendezvous with the Sun, *Ulysses* was being granted a third flight at the exact moment when I decided to write again and extend this journey of my own, and when I heard this on the news I burst out laughing and was dumbfounded, and I felt as though I was the one who'd just been granted an extension, and I no longer knew what to think, the whole thing was beyond me, yes, how on earth could my destiny be so closely linked, or in any case synchronized, with that of a little probe weighing fifty-seven kilos? It was weird and scary, in a way, and I called Sophie to fill her in on this latest coincidence and to say that it seemed like a stretch,* even to me, and no one would ever believe me, and dryly she asked what else I'd been doing since I was eight years old but stretching reality and adding its scalps to my belt, and I had no business complaining and she looked forward to seeing me, and hanging up I wondered whether, by any chance, she might possibly weigh fifty-seven kilos exactly. This was the case.

---

* Literally, "*tiré par les cheveux*" (pulled by the hair).

McNally Editions reissues books that are not widely known but have stood the test of time, that remain as singular and engaging as when they were written. Available in the US wherever books are sold or by subscription from mcnallyeditions.com.